Green and Profitable

BOOKS 1-4

Shel Horowitz

Green and Profitable Books 1-4
©2015, Shel Horowitz

ISBN-13: 978-1511420006
ISBN-10: 1511420006

Printed in the United States of America
10, 9, 8, 7, 6, 5, 4, 3, 2

Published by AWM Books - Hadley, MA

Contents

BOOK 3: POLICY AND ETHICS ISSUES FOR GREEN BUSINESSES

BOOK 4: THE NEW REALITIES OF 21ST-CENTURY BUSINESS

Green and
Profitable

BOOK 1

Profitable Green Business Practices

Shel Horowitz

This Major Paper Company Has Been **Recycling Since 1950**

 Would you believe...a household paper products company that switched to recycled raw materials in 1950, and has been producing recycled paper towels, napkins, toilet paper, and tissues ever since? A company that was so dedicated to creating "paper made from paper, not from trees"(TM) that it actually set up its own paper collection service (and currently collects paper for recycling from a 300-mile radius)? A company that saw no reason to jack up prices and has remained a consistent player in the lower price points? And a company that did this with such humility that *it didn't bother telling the public for decades*, and didn't make a big deal about it until 2009?

Yes, this company exists. Marcal, founded in 1932, went to manufacturing its paper products from recycled paper nearly 60 years ago. Small mentions had crept into the packing by the early 1990s—but only when turnaround CEO Tim Spring and several other executives were hired to bring the company back from bankruptcy in 2008 did the company realize it was sitting on a marketing goldmine. The following year, Marcal launched its Small Steps(TM) consumer brand, aimed squarely at environmentally conscious consumers. Not only is it 100% recycled, but the manufacturing process does not use chlorine bleach, the products are hypoallergenic and nearly lint-free

We could save a full million trees if every American household bought just a single roll of recycled paper towels, box of recycled tissues, or package of napkins, the company says.

What does that mean specifically? Every year, saving a million trees would:

✓ Keep 250 million pounds of carbon dioxide out of the air while adding 260 million pounds of oxygen (enough to supply 520 million people)

✓ Absorb as much carbon as is produced by a million cars each driving 26,000 miles

✓ Substantially reduce methane emissions (potentially a bigger problem than CO2) from landfills, compared to using virgin paper

As a consumer, I became aware of recycled paper in the early 1970s, and started looking for suppliers. At that time it was very hard to find any paper identified as recycled, and even harder to find recycled paper that was high enough quality and low enough price to make the switch worth it.

In the past ten or fifteen years, it's gotten much easier. I now buy exclusively recycled paper not only for household products (where prices are comparable to standard brands) but also for my office printers (where I have to pay substantially more). When

I think of how much Marcal recycled paper I would have bought in the decades starting from when I became aware until the market finally caught up, I have to wonder what took them so long.

Considering that in the few months following its introduction, Small Steps, which is in about 50 percent of US markets, has become the top-selling recycled brand, Marcal executives must be wondering the same thing. (It just proves the case I make in my eighth book Guerrilla Marketing Goes Green: Winning Strategies to Improve Your Profits and Your Planet—that it's not enough to *be* a Green company, you also have to tell the world.)

Marcal is even beginning to gather signatures on this nice little eco-pledge:

- ✓ I am only one person.
  But what I do impacts the whole world.

- ✓ I have decided that the health of the earth is important to me.
  I have decided to honor this priority in small ways.

- ✓ If I can share a ride or take public transportation to help save the air, I will.

- ✓ If I can make everyday choices that help save energy, I will.

- ✓ If I can choose recycled paper that help save the forests and wildlife habitats, I will.

The company is promoting the pledge through social media, appearances by its spokesperson, and through a link on its community page. I signed, and I hope you will too. Meanwhile, I've been buying Small Steps, and can report that the quality is fine.

Incidentally, in the new book, I discuss ways companies can protect themselves from accusations of greenwashing. One of those is to state honestly that you've been using recycled materials for 30 years. By 2010, Marcal was able to double that claim.

(Special thanks to Lindsay Jacob of Marcal for supplying a lot of raw material I used in researching this article.)

Some **Big Companies** Going **Green and Profitable**

In the corporate world, if you start talking about going green, you'll often hear messages like this:

> "Yes, we're going green, despite the expense.
> It's the right thing to do."

Yes, it is the right thing to do. And yes, very small companies are often nimble enough to seize the combined economic and environmental advantages.

But smart companies of any size can go green in ways that are highly profitable. Even large, slow-moving companies can save enormously.

Want some examples?

Southwest Airlines

Southwest expanded its on-plane and in-terminal recycling program from just aluminum cans to a much wider assortment of recycled materials. Working with a vendor who is able to handle co-mingled recyclables—which means no extra burden on flight attendants who would find it difficult to collect paper, plastic, and aluminum separately—the company is slashing a big chunk out of its multimillion dollar annual waste disposal budget.

And, as Southwest spokesperson Laurel Moffat notes, "To date, we have saved more than 37,000 trees, more than one million gallons of oil, and more than 15 million gallons of water."

For in-terminal recycling, the two airports piloting the program are diverting 12 to 19 container loads out of the waste stream every month.

Google

The company's big, powerful servers not only hold and instantly organize much of the world's knowledge, but consume enormous quantities of electricity. Google has invested in a massive project to develop a 350-mile-long 6,000-megawatt wind-powered electrical backbone off the North Atlantic Coast of the United States—that's enough to power 1.9 million households. Stretching from  Virginia to New Jersey, these connected turbines are well-located to ease power burdens on New York, Newark, Philadelphia, Wilmington, Baltimore, and Washington.

Using the backbone model will eliminate the need to build individual transmission lines from each offshore wind project, and thus reduce the number of permits and environmental impact studies—and bring the wind plants on line much sooner.

According to Rick Needham, Google's Green Business Operations Director, the company is providing 37.5 percent of the initial-stage equity. And profit is most definitely one of Google's motives: "We believe in investing in projects that make good business sense and further the development of renewable energy. We're willing to take calculated risks on early stage ideas and projects that can have dramatic impacts while offering attractive returns," Needham says.

The Empire State Building

New York's most famous skyscraper is shaving $4.4 million a year in energy costs—40 percent of its former $11 million annual energy bills—in a major "deep energy retrofit" that involves upgrading every single one of its 6,514 windows. For roughly $700 per window—versus $2500 each to completely replace them—each window is cleaned, coated with a thin UV-resistant film, and insulated with pressurized argon and krypton gasses. Other parts of the renovation include insulating the radiators, using both natural and artificial lighting more efficiently, wireless and portable thermostat sensors, and occupancy sensors that prevent heating or cooling of unused space. The building is also switching to individual tenant-by-tenant metering, meaning those who leave appliances and lights on when no one is using them will pay the cost of the wasted electricity.

Building manager and co-owner Anthony Malkin points out that buildings account for 80 percent of the city's energy use, and not in equal numbers. "Even more interestingly, 20 percent of the buildings consume 80 percent of that energy. So 64 percent of all energy consumed in New York City is consumed by 20 percent of the buildings. That really took me by surprise."

This project could easily be replicated elsewhere, because the impact on profitability is huge. Look at the numbers: The project cost is $13.2 million, and the annual return (savings) is $4.4 million. That means the first 3 years pay for the project (that's an ROI of 33% a year). And the second three years put an extra $13.2 million into profit! With banks paying a measly 1.07 percent on a one-year and 2.3 percent return even on a 5-year CD right now, a 33 percent return is mighty attractive.

How much oil and coal could we eliminate, and how much capital would be freed up for job creation, if every company took just one of its buildings through a deep-energy retrofit process?

Going Green: Private Sector Must Take Up the Slack

Many observers in the environmental movement were dispirited by the US election results in November [2010], with the election of several prominent climate-change deniers and the power switch in the House of Representatives.

Political reality around sustainability varies a lot with location. Western Europe has been pushing hard on green technology leadership for years, combining business and government to drive the change. From simple innovations like a light/heavy switch for toilet flushes  to the complexities of generating significant power from offshore and mountaintop wind farms, Europe has made it clear that carbon reduction and energy and water conservation are priorities. China, using an approach dictated largely by government policy, has become a world leader in solar.

However, both the European and Chinese systems send out mixed messages. Europe relies far too heavily on dangerous and un-green nuclear power; China has made an even larger commitment to dirty, health-killing coal.

In many parts of Africa and Asia, NGOs and nonprofits—often more than government or private industry—are taking the lead, bringing low-cost and highly portable energy technologies in to disadvantaged villages, replacing polluting, unsafe, and carbon-spewing kerosene, wood, and charcoal with clean alternatives—decentralized to the level of a single home.

Turning back to the US: I believe the election shows that Americans can't rely on the federal government to deal with climate change on our behalf; as business leaders and thought leaders, we have to do it ourselves. Nothing meaningful will come out of Washington for the next two gridlocked years, on climate change, going green, or many other issues.

But this doesn't mean the work will stop. Not at all.

Individuals within companies will continue to spearhead the movement for change, and those companies will slowly turn to embrace the change. Individuals within households will continue to make better choices for themselves and their families, and the machinery of commerce will continue to make those choices ever more widely available and affordable.

First, of course, is the pioneering work done for the past several decades by companies that were founded with a strong environmental chromosome. When companies like Whole Foods or Ben & Jerry's take steps to go more green, it's totally in keeping with the corporate culture—the company DNA—and with the needs and desires of their customer base.

But wider change must be driven by companies considered much more mainstream. "Fringe" businesses—small innovative concerns that will grow to become the Whole Foods and Ben & Jerry's of the future—may show us how to get there, but to really make a difference, much bigger players have to get involved.

Will this happen without government carrots? Actually, it's happening already. Let's take Walmart as an example. The largest retailer in the world—that sounds pretty mainstream. Founded by a conservative, pickup-driving rural American from the South (the most conservative region in the country), Walmart certainly doesn't kowtow to tree-huggers. In fact, it's often been criticized by environmentalists for a host of issues ranging from store siting to labor practices.

Yet in the last few years, starting with the appointment of Lee Scott as CEO and continuing past his term, Walmart has taken numerous major steps toward sustainability in both its operations and its product line. Why?

> **1.** Walmart's always been awesome at slashing the cost and boosting the efficiency of its logistics. So the dozens of green operations initiatives that actually save the company millions of dollars are a no-brainer. Examples range from fitting its long-haul trucks with separate temperature systems so the big diesels don't have to run just to heat or cool the cab, to switching to LED parking lot lighting in some stores—which slashed energy consumption by 48 percent and maintenance costs by 75 percent—to saving 678,000 barrels of oil and 290,000 metric tons of greenhouse gases a year just by cutting plastic shopping bag waste by a third.

2. The company realized that bringing in green product lines (from energy-efficient light bulbs to organic food to healthy cleaning and body care lines) opened up enormous revenue and profit potential.

In other words, the company realized it could both save a fortune and make a fortune. So what's not to like? And this is the future of going green in the US for the next two years: companies stepping forward to do the right thing out of economic self-interest.

Of course, if the Obama administration had engaged in a massive Marshall Plan-style program to create hundreds of thousands of jobs by converting to green power sources, we might not need to ask ourselves how to move forward without the government's help. But that's a topic for a different column.

Sustainability Innovators
Around the World

Every once in a while, I'll devote this column to a roundup of some of the coolest sustainability initiatives I've come across anywhere in the world. This is the first installment, featuring five different ventures on five different continents, and business models that include an architect working solo, a manufacturing corporation, a nonprofit, and a couple of small companies.

United States
Kenguru—Sustainable Independence for Wheelchair Users

Think about how many resources are consumed by a standard wheelchair van. A huge vehicle with complicated, slow, hydraulic lifts: expensive in both money and materials to build, and consuming huge amounts of fuel to operate.

Now...reinvent the whole thing: a one-person electric vehicle, tiny, secure, and empowering the wheelchair user to control his or her own transportation. The user rolls in up a ramp through a rear hatch facing the curb, fastens the chair, and then it's off to work, play, or whatever. www.kenguru.com

Australia
Freemantle Timber Traders—Turning Old Buildings Into New Building Materials

This company has designed its own tools to salvage lumber from demolition projects in ways it claims provides much cleaner, more intact hardwood lumber than conventional demolition and salvage techniques. If the greenest building is the one that's already been built, the next-greenest might be the one that uses materials from buildings that existed and were taken down. www.fremantletimbertraders.com.au/profile.asp, community page at www.facebook.com/environmentaltimber.

Hong Kong
Gary Chang Maximizes Every Inch of 344-square foot Apartment

This may be the tiniest apartment in the world to have full kitchen and bath, a well-equipped bar, guest quarters, and 24 rooms (though not all at the same time). Using movable walls, foldable surfaces, and other tricks, this ingenious architect shows that it's possible to live quite luxuriously in a very small space. At one time, there were seven people living there! Buckminster Fuller would be proud. Video tour (two minutes):

blogs.wsj.com/developments/2010/04/28/hong-kong-architect-crams-24-rooms-into-344-square-feet/

United States
Evocative Design—Who Needs Styrofoam Peanuts When You've Got Mushrooms?

It's hard to imagine too many products less environmentally friendly than Styrofoam. Even experienced plastics recyclers usually can't figure out what to do it. And, in my personal opinion, it ruins the taste of food or hot drinks stored in it.

A whole lot of Styrofoam gets turned into packing peanuts. And even if you have good intentions and take them down to your local shipping store to reuse, some of them always get away and get stepped on, wedged into things, or become a nuisance in other ways.

So why not avoid the problem in the first place and find a natural, compostable packing material? Evocative Design offers packing made from cottonseed and buckwheat hulls, held together with filaments made from mushroom roots—while saving 85 percent of the energy and reducing 90 percent of the carbon dioxide compared with Styrofoam.

planetforward.ca/blog/packing-peanuts-meet-a-replacement-that-is-grown-from-mushrooms/

Burkina Faso (and three other African countries): Association la Voute Nubienne Creates Timberless Housing

Deforestation is a huge problem in sub-Saharan Africa, and the loss of forest often leads to desertification—exacerbating hunger and other social ills in the process. Cross-pollinating a vaulted-roof housing construction technique from the Nubian culture in Egypt (on the other side of the continent) with local labor and non-wood earth

bricks made from local materials, a French nonprofit has been building sustainable homes and community buildings, and creating jobs. The houses cost only about $100 each to build, and make a real difference in these economically marginal communities. There is a bit of plastic sheeting involved in waterproofing the roof, but the house can be built without sheet metal and without timber supports, unlike the usual building styles in the Sahel region.

An English-language page about the construction technique is at www.lavoutenubienne.org/-The-VN-Technical-Solution; if you'd like to donate, the group is set up with Global Giving at www.globalgiving.org/projects/help-build-sustainable-africa-houses/people/.

Easy **Money-Saving**
Green Tips for Business

Environmental measures can be easy or hard. Go for the easy stuff with the biggest return first. For example:

Most businesses leak huge quantities of heated air in the winter and cooled air in the summer. **Simple and very inexpensive measures like insulating outlets and switchplates with foam gaskets** (and plugging unused outside-wall outlets with baby outlet protectors) on outside-facing walls can make an immediate difference. So can making sure windows are properly caulked. And ensuring that doors to the outside close tightly and have weatherstripping and heat-trapping rubber sweeps.

Install programmable thermostats to stop heating/cooling air when the building is shut for the night—and program them properly: no more than 68° F/ 20° C in the winter, no lower than 75° F/24° C in the summer during working hours, and perhaps 55° F/13° C in the winter and 85° F/29° C in the summer, from half an hour after the end of the workday until half an hour before employees start arriving in the morning.

Plug computers, machinery, and appliances into smart power strips that eliminate "energy vampires" by cutting power to the device when it's not in use—and train your people to flip the power strips off if they're the last to leave at night.

Cut your paper costs by 40 percent or so by switching to duplexing (two-sided) printers and copiers, setting them to default to two-sided, and training your employees to use that setting when possible. Have a goal that the only single-sided copies are the last pages of documents with an odd number of pages. The amount of paper that can be saved will shock you.

Of course, some few documents do need to be printed one-sided. But often, that's because they're going to be used as a reprint master—which can be avoided by printing from a digital file instead of a hard copy, gaining higher quality in the process.

Encourage employees to do more on screen and print less in the first place. Demonstrate the computer settings that display larger print without changing the actual document (for instance, the View-Zoom feature in Microsoft Word and most Internet browsing software)—this makes reading on the screen a lot more comfortable, and printing a lot less necessary.

Recycle all the scrap paper in your office. Recycle plastic and metal as well. And switch to recycled copy paper, toilet paper, and paper towels; these days, the latter two don't have to cost any more than non-recycled, and copy paper is only a bit more.

Change your break room and lounges around with a goal of sustainability: Get rid of disposable cups and buy each employee a personalized coffee mug, plus a few for visitors. Use reusable rags and sponges instead of paper towels. Switch to organic fair-trade coffee, tea, and cocoa. If your business is in a place where the water is drinkable, add a water filter to the sink and educate your employees that using filtered tap water is much greener than bottled, as well as much cheaper for them.

Partner with a local organic farm to offer a once-a-week farmers market in your parking lot or on a lawn, where employees can stock up on fresh organic veggies—this costs you nothing, and your people will love it (especially if they live in cities).

Switch to natural/organic pest control and landscaping.

Install an aerator on every faucet.

Prohibit smoking on your campus—but first, announce the deadline,  and in the meantime, provide smoking-cessation assistance for employees who need it. (You'll pay for the program through savings in reduced absesm for health reasons, and possibly lower insurance costs. You may also be able to get grant funding or tap into no-cost quit-smoking programs.)

Next, look at steps you can take to make your employees more comfortable and happier, which in turn will make them more productive. Bring houseplants into work areas—they chew up carbon dioxide (a major greenhouse gas) and turn it into oxygen. Provide natural lighting where possible. Use fresh air from open windows during the spring and fall, if your building is set up with windows that open. Use curtains and drapes to let in sun in the winter, block it out during the hot summer—and to keep heat in during winter nights, while releasing it in summer.

These, of course, are only the tip of the iceberg. We can all cut energy, water, and waste in thousands of ways, many of which, like the measures above, cost little or nothing.

Set aside the money you save from these measures to look at more complex steps, such as adding more insulation, auditing your manufacturing process for energy savings, switching to low-water or even waterless toilets, planting an area of your roof or adding solar panels, going through the LEED or EnergyStar certification process, and so on.

And don't forget to start talking about all the green things you're doing in your marketing, on your website, and in your press releases. The marketing benefit alone in some cases, can be enough to cover the capital cost of the next round of improvements.

A **Whole Country** that Runs on **Renewable Energy**

I've known for years that Iceland is a geothermal paradise, so when we went there this summer, I made sure to pay some attention to the power supply.

As it turned out, that was absurdly easy to do. You can't travel in Iceland without encountering the power of geothermal energy, and many Icelanders we met bragged about their geothermal systems. We even encountered several museum exhibits highlighting volcanic and geothermal activity.

 We visited a geothermal power plant that contained an energy museum. We cooked eggs in a geothermal spring, and tasted bread that had been baked in the ground, overnight.

While there is significant use of hydropower along with geothermal, we saw almost no solar in Iceland—in part because usually they don't have too much sun, and in part because geothermal and hydro readily available and produce much steadier (and cheaper) power.

In the United States, where I live, harnessing geothermal typically involves drilling below the earth to a layer with year-round consistent temperature at about 50°F/10°C, and tapping into that layer to boost heating in the winter, and cooling in the summer. I live in the northeast United States, in a region called New England, where temperatures typically range from -5°F/-20.5°C on a cold winter night to around 95°F/35°C on a sunny, hot summer afternoon. And in fact, my neighbors just put in a geothermal system, in their house built in 1747. Like most geothermal installations in the US, they are using the thermal power directly, to heat and cool water.

In actively volcanic Iceland, it's a different story. Temperatures in many of the hot springs are hot enough to kill a person quickly, approaching the boiling point of water (212°F/100°C).

All you have to do is feel the temperature of the water coming out of the hot tap to know that geothermal means something different in Iceland. It's HOT! As hot as the solar-heated water I use in my home, which is to say hotter than any tap water I've encountered from fossil-heated sources. Our water is so hot that we warn our guests about how not to scald themselves in the shower. So that aspect of Iceland felt very familiar.

There are several differences, though:

First, the water at home smells of the chlorine that municipal authorities use to purify it. In many parts of Iceland, including the capital, Reykjavík, the water smells strongly of sulfur—so strongly that my toothbrush would smell like elderly eggs, hours after brushing.

Another difference is the ubiquity of the system. Geothermal is heavily commercialized in Iceland. Municipalities harness and pipe it into virtually every house and building, as well as the numerous geothermally heated municipal swimming pools and hot tubs (up to 111°F/44°C) that were in literally every town we visited—one of the few bargains in a rather expensive country, where practically everything else

has to be imported. But in the US, geothermal systems are purchased by the individual homeowner, and are expensive enough that people are very cautious about making such a large investment. My neighbors spent $38,000 on their system.

And fourth, I was surprised at how much geothermal power is used to create steam and spin turbines to generate electricity, and how much of that electricity is transported across significant distances; I'd expected most of it to be heating water for direct use rather than spinning turbines, and to be used near the point of origin, as it is at home. Transporting energy across distances cuts down on efficiency.

But efficiency and conservation aren't such big concerns in Iceland. We were rather surprised that saving water or electricity didn't seem to be a value. People just ran the water or left lights on. Their attitude was that they had plenty, it was really cheap, and they didn't have to worry about running out.

Personally, I think that's shortsighted. They may have plenty now, but that could change in the future, especially as the country begins exporting to parts of Europe that are not so richly endowed with power. I think the conservation-isn't-important attitude will change with education and a values shift, just as it has shifted in Asia, North America, and especially continental Europe. Meanwhile, Iceland can truly claim to have one of the greenest power grids in the world.

In a country with only 318,452 inhabitants and approximately 116,000 households as of January 2011, this tiny country has the capacity to supply much of Europe's energy needs. In fact, plans are afoot to build deep-sea cables that will export as much as 5 billion kilowatt-hours of clean, renewable electricity to the rest of Europe—enough to power 1.25 million homes. Those of you based in Europe, especially, should be on the lookout for opportunities to profit from this coming industrial shift. And those in other seismically active parts of the world might want to think about how to get your country into massive geothermal.

As Green Gets More **Complex**... It Also Gets **Easier**

As a long-term marketer, media-watcher and journalist, I learned long ago that you can tell a whole lot about market trends, as well as the thinking and feeling patterns of not just the overall culture but also the cultures of subgroups within niches—just by studying the ads aimed at them. And you can find out a great deal about people's hot buttons and how to persuade.

When large corporations pay good money to display an ad, it means their research shows their customers want to buy the sorts of products, services, or ideas described in those ads, and that at least a percentage of them will respond to the types of language, graphics, and offers that those ads encompass.

Here's an example directly related to the green world:

I'm looking at a magazine published by McGraw-Hill, about as mainstream a publisher as you can find. The magazine, called GreenSource: The Magazine of Sustainable Design, is aimed at green architects, designers, and builders.

Firstly, it says a great deal that the green design and construction niche is big enough to get attention from a publisher like McGraw-Hill, and that this magazine seems to have no trouble finding advertisers, even in a down economy.

And secondly, by looking at the ads, I'm reminded that the bar has gone sharply higher for sustainable design over the past few years. Going green, and being able to convince a skeptical green consumer base that you've done so, is a lot deeper now than simply using recycled materials, driving a hybrid, or caulking all the drafty spaces. All sorts of new issues are coming into play. Layers of complexity I never would have dreamed would become mainstream factors are now being talked about every day.

Here are just the ads in the first eight pages (before the Table of Contents):

The first is a two-page ad is for recycled ceiling panels. And joining the trend toward making claims believable by quantifying them, the ad claims 100 million pounds of old ceiling tiles were reclaimed, keeping 50,000 tons of them out of landfills. These two numbers happen to be equivalent—perhaps the copywriter wasn't sure which would have greater impact, and so used both.

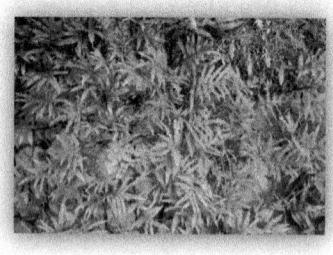

Turning the page—another two-page ad, for a "living wall": "biofilter technology [that] not only captures airborne pollutants, it breaks them down." The pictures show a standing forest on the left, a multistory building wall covered with plants on the right.

The outer half of the next page has a half-page vertical ad for "vertical landscaping" (appropriately enough). It shows plants growing thickly on the outside of a two-story townhouse. The inner half of the page is the magazine's masthead. Opposite, a full-page ad for "the only gypsum board that clears the air." This one claims to permanently remove Volatile Organic Compounds (VOCs) for up to 75 years.

On the next page, another half-page vertical for "drivable grass®"—a driveway paving replacement that allows storm water to drain through to the soil underneath. And opposite that, a full-page ad for a low-emissions certification agency.

The last ad before the contents page is for an aluminum building material with 70- to 80 percent post-consumer recycled content, and ISO certification to prove it.

Walls that filter rather than emit pollutants, and paving solutions that recycle the rainwater—were these the kinds of things you expected to be dealing with when you decided to take your company green? I didn't think so. It all sounds so complicated!

But consider the positive side: if this level of awareness is becoming so common that these are the advertisers in the prized (and expensive) front-of-the-book pages at a major-publisher magazine, *that creates a huge opening for you to push for greater sustainability measures in your company.* You can use this kind of magazine to prove to the powers-that-be that the world isn't standing still, and that your organization needs to both be doing more on sustainability, and finding ways to convey that commitment to the public.

And that may turn out to be a very exciting task.

What's the **Right Clean Energy Solution** for You?

So, you've made the decision to convert all or part of your energy use to clean, renewable sources? Congratulations on a great decision—but now how do you decide among all these alternatives: various forms of solar, wind, hydro, geothermal, as well as more exotic formats like magnetic and tidal? The choice may seem bewildering.

These two principles may help you figure it out. First, do conservation first, and second, pick the best alternative based on conditions on-site.

Conservation First

Energy you save outright is energy you don't need to generate or harvest. As one very prominent example, New York City's iconic Empire State Building enlisted the Rocky Mountain Institute and other groups to design and implement a "deep energy retrofit" that's saving over $4 million every year. While the $13 million investment was not cheap, the 33% annual ROI far outpaces any conventional investment vehicle and will continue to pay multimillion dollar dividends for decades.

Not every business has the capital for that kind of program. But the good news is every business can find ways to save at least a few percentage points on up to as much as 80 percent of energy consumption. Whether the investment is small or large, the payback can be quick (and the savings reinvested in more energy conservation). If you only need half as much power as you did before, you can put in a smaller and cheaper alternative energy system.

Conservation can be as simple as turning off unneeded lights and computers or as complex as completely redesigning and rebuilding an industrial process. Do an energy audit with a consultant who can see not just the usual incremental measures but also the potential for sweeping, big-picture changes. For the Empire State Building, that actually meant temporarily converting a floor of the building into a factory to convert the old windows into highly efficient ones, on-site (among other improvements).

Find the Right Alternative

Once you've reduced your energy footprint through conservation, it's time to research your alternative energy options. When possible, generate the power you need as close to the point of use as you can. Enormous quantities of energy get wasted in transmission and transportation of energy, so it will almost always be better to produce on-site. Thus, a rooftop solar array or ground-level wind turbine makes more sense in most cases than piping in electricity from a photovoltaic farm hundreds of kilometers away.

Each energy system is going to be better suited to some installations than others. Factoring in any grants and tax incentives, how many years can you expect for payback, and thus what is your ROI?

Without in any way trying to substitute for a professional evaluation, here at least are some quick guidelines:

Solar

Is it sunny more often than cloudy? Do you have adequate exposure: an area that gets good sun and is not in the shadow of a tall building, a mountain, or a tree canopy? If looking at rooftops, will your roof support the added weight of solar infrastructure? If  looking at ground installation, can you install the system so as to permit other uses (for example, an employee community garden) underneath? Do you have a vehicle fleet that could be converted to solar and used to recharge the grid? Do you have room and budget for both solar thermal (e.g., hot water) and photovoltaic (electricity generation), and if not, which should you do first?

Wind

Does your location have steady but relatively modest wind—fast enough to spin the blades, but not so fast that it tears the system apart in a year or two? Will your neighbors put up a big fight that makes the project too expensive and uncomfortable? Have you looked into less intrusive systems such as low-to-the-ground vertical-axis turbines?

Hydro

Are you sited near a river or stream? Can you use technology that captures energy from the moving water directly, or will you need to build a dam? If you're damming a body of water, have you fully analyzed the environmental impact? Can you use the water to directly run a

mill, or will you be using it to generate electricity?

Geothermal

Do you have enough land to put in a system? Can you harness that energy for enough uses (space heating and cooling, water heating) to justify the substantial capital cost? Do you live in Iceland, where your energy is already geothermal?

Contributing to the Solution

Whichever technology turns out to be right for your location, moving toward clean renewables is a great move. Installing a system that's right for your site will lower your energy costs and carbon footprint, while contributing at least a little bit toward preventing catastrophic climate change. So do your part—but "do it smart."

One **Product**, Multiple **Benefits**

Do more with less—makes sense when you're thinking green, doesn't it—especially when you let it expand your idea of what's possible.

A guiding principle in thinking green is to achieve multiple purposes with a single item. The item could be a product, a component, a service, or maybe even an idea. Systems that incorporate this principle are generally much more sustainable, need fewer components, and are therefore also more economical.

Does that sound like a bunch of abstractions that's a bit too complicated to puzzle out? Let's look at some specific examples.

Purus Pavers: Old Soda Bottles Solve Water Runoff Problems

Green builders are discovering eco-friendly substitutes for the traditional asphalt paving area. Asphalt prevents water from seeping into the ground and diverts it—usually into sewers, but sometimes into places where it causes harmful erosion.

By contrast, a paving system that allows the water to drain back into the ground right there and yet insulates vehicles from the problems of parking or driving directly on the ground can maintain the water table, reduce concentrations of toxic contaminants, eliminate the erosion problem, and even allow for plantings that grow close to the ground—thus adding oxygen and reducing CO_2 emissions, which in turn help preserve the earth in the face of catastrophic climate change.

These pavers create a latticework of support above an open area, so the water can freely drain, right where the rain falls.

I've seen concrete pavers like this, and they're very cool. A company called Purus <www.purus-plastics.de/en/ecorasterr/ecorasterr-s50.html> decided to take things up a notch, and make the pavers out of recycled polyethylene from old soda bottles. This adds several more benefits: longer lasting landfills, avoiding toxic fumes from incineration of plastic (which should NEVER be burned), reuse of materials, among others.

Ocean Arks International: Waste Becomes Raw Material in a Closed Loop

Instead of the typical open system where an industrial process creates waste that is released into the environment, enviro-pioneer John Todd keeps asking how we can close the loop by using that waste as an input for something else.

After all, that's what happens in nature: humans and other animals breathe in oxygen and breathe out carbon dioxide, while plants breathe in that carbon dioxide and breathe oxygen back out. A dead tree becomes habitat for nesting birds, and when the birds die, their nutrients are absorbed back into the soil where plants can use them.

The company Todd founded, <u>Ocean Arks International</u>, takes this single simple idea in amazing directions. For instance, an integrated system of businesses and activities called The Intervale <<u>www.intervale.org/</u>>, in Burlington, Vermont, uses brewery waste to grow mushrooms, mushroom waste to feed fish, fish waste to grow hydroponic vegetables, and so on

Expanding the principle again, Todd and his colleagues design and build restorative ecosystems that reduce carbon, digest human-caused waste, and revivify dead or dying bodies of water. (<u>Click here to read more about John Todd's work</u>)

Organic and Biodynamic Farming: Benefiting All Stakeholders

The last example is one that most of us are familiar with: organic farming, and its more tightly regulated cousin, Demeter Certified Biodynamic agriculture <<u>www.demeterbta.com/</u>>.

You already know that organic foods not only eliminate harmful chemicals but also typically produce tastier foods. But you might not know that organic agriculture can sequester 7000 pounds of carbon per acre...that agriculture can raise a significant portion of our energy needs through oilseed crops like sunflowers (yes, I'm aware there are issues in using cropland for energy)...that a good organic diet of grasses and flax can significantly reduce the (very troubling greenhouse gas) methane emissions from cow burps...and that a cow fed an organic diet will be far more profitable for farmers, because she is likely to live up to three times as long, have many more lactation cycles, and even yield 20 percent more beef. (These statistics are taken from my report on the 2011 Sustainable Foods Summit held in San Francisco: <greenandprofitable.com/its-about-tradeoffs-part-1/>).

And You?

These are just three of thousands of examples. How can you incorporate holistic, systemic thinking to create multiple benefits with one innovation?

Green as **Sexy**

As a good follow-up to last month's column on marketing green products to nongreen audience, let's take things a notch higher.

As you read this, I'm off to Houston, Texas, USA, to give a speech called "Making Green Sexy" at a green buildings conference.

The interesting thing about that idea is that "sexy" is in the eye of the beholder—which is a good thing for those of us who don't look like supermodels and still manage to have loving relationships.

Last month, I mentioned the Tesla roadster, something that would fit most people's definition of sexy. It's a super-sporty car, full of Coke-bottle curves. It screams speed, power, luxury, and high status. (If you don't know what it looks like, you can see pictures at http://www.teslamotors.com/roadster). It also happens to be the most high-performance electric car that's ever been out on the market.

Yes, I'll be showing a picture of the Tesla roadster in my talk in Texas. But I'll also show a picture of Amory Lovins' ultra-efficient house (built back in 1983 in the Colorado Rockies), which is not what most people would define as sexy—at least until they look closely.

What makes Lovins' home sexy is not its looks—which are unusual, and certainly not in keeping with today's styles (though certainly reasonably attractive to my eyes). Rather, this is what I find sexy about it:

✓ Despite the cold, snowy winters and hot, sunny summers in the Aspen, Colorado snowbelt (one of the downhill skiing capitals of the United States), this house has neither a furnace nor an air conditioner—because it doesn't need either one.

✓ The sunroom is warm enough, even during the winter, that Lovins actually grows bananas inside.

✓ At 4000 square feet/371.6 square meters, it's big enough to compare with the grand mansions that we popularly think of as sexy.

✓ Because expensive items like heating and cooling systems weren't purchased, the extra-cost green and sustainable energy features paid for themselves in just 10 months.

✓ As a passive solar home, much of the energy savings was achieved by thinking, designing, and building holistically, where a single component might achieve multiple goals; he referred to one arch in his house that accomplishes 12 different functions.

✓ Long before the term "cradle-to-cradle" came into use, this house was designed to close as many loops as possible, and to produce almost no waste.

✓ Even using 1983 technology, which we in the solar and green world would consider quite primitive by today's standards, the house makes nearly all of its own electricity (when I heard Lovins speak several years ago, he said he averaged a USD $5 electric bill for the residential portion of his home/office—and even if higher energy prices have brought that up to, say, $25, that's still quite remarkable).

What's really sexy to me about the Lovins house is not even the individual features. It's the potential for world-wide planet-saving. Think about what kind of world we'd be living in right now if for the past 29 years since Lovins proved it was feasible, most houses had been built along these lines.

✓ Atmospheric carbon would be greatly reduced—probably well below the 350 parts-per-million danger zone that we are now exceeding—and thus, global warming would not be a desperate situation.

✓ Pollution from burning fossil fuels (and from extracting them from the earth) would be a tiny fraction of what it is now, and this in turn would mean sharply reduced healthcare costs—because a lot fewer people would be getting sick.

✓ Because there would be no need for the world's largest economies to chase after oil reserves, foreign policy would have been reshaped—away from wars over energy resources and toward inspiring real democracy and economic self-sufficiency

✓ And finally, all that capital that's been spent on buying energy would have been freed up to invest elsewhere causing a flowering of technology and the arts, and a massive rise in living standards around the world.

This kind of world should have been our inheritance. Let's at least make it our legacy.

Simple and **Elegant Solutions** to Complex **Environmental Problems**

If your goal is to let astronauts write in deep space, you could spend millions of dollars researching, designing, and prototyping pens that will work without gravity—or you could simply hand out a box of pencils. Maybe they could even be special pencils that make a deeper, darker writing imprint and don't fade quickly (such pencils already exist).

Just as in the space program, in the world of complex environmental problems, the best solution is often surprisingly simple and very elegant. And we as green business people need to find those solutions, bring them to consumers—and market their benefits.

The massive consumer products company Procter & Gamble understands this concept and has capitalized on it. Company engineers realized that one of the biggest consumers of energy in households is heating water, and one of the largest uses of hot water is laundry. You could attack that problem with complex solutions such as heating the water with solar systems—or you could market a detergent that works perfectly well in cold water.

P&G chose the latter course, and developed Tide Coldwater, which it actively markets both as a green product to the green market, and as a money-saving product for the general consumer market. If you visit www.tidecoldwater.com on a Flash-enabled computer, the first thing you get is a calculator that allows US residents to figure out exactly how much they'd save by washing in cold water, state by state, according to their own laundry habits.

Of course, you don't really need Tide Coldwater for these savings. I find that my clothes come out just fine in cold water, using a store brand high-efficiency liquid detergent. But P&G's marketing for this brand has focused heavily on the green benefits, and they are reaching a lot of people who had been using hot water to wash.

However, the big lesson here is the simple and elegant solution. For the average householder, it's going to be far cheaper to reduce water heating energy by 30 percent or so than to install a greener hot water system. For tenants who would never pony up a big capital investment to improve a property they don't own, cold-water washing is an extremely sensible choice.

In my latest book, **Guerrilla Marketing Goes Green**, I discuss in some detail the work of two practical visionaries who are really good at solving complex problems with simple elegance: John Todd and Amory Lovins.

Decades before most people had ever heard of concepts like "zero waste" and "cradle-to-cradle," Todd grasped the simple and elegant concept that the waste from one production process could almost always be raw material for another one. And you can create an ecosystem of several of these processes layered together.

Thus, spent grain at a brewery turns out to be a perfect growing medium for commercial mushroom production, and that in turn generates a very nice fish food. He has used this single insight to develop biological systems that actually clean and restore polluted wetlands, rivers, and lakes. Another of his innovations in water purification is a simple tube running through the desert that uses the natural range of temperature conditions to sterilize safe drinking water in a refugee camp, no chemicals needed.

For Lovins, the three simple and elegant ideas are:

1) You can design for such deep conservation that you don't need to buy big expensive systems like furnaces and air conditioners—and the savings on these capital costs, along with the savings on energy, pay for the improvements. He has designed homes that didn't need heating or air conditioning in climates ranging from the deep-winter Colorado Rocky Mountains (where his own 1983 home is a showplace for what's possible) to places where temperatures exceeding 100°F/40°C are common.

2) Enormous amounts of energy is wasted in transmission losses. If you generate power where you need it, you need considerably less than if you transport it across great distances.

3) One design component can achieve multiple purposes.

Here are a few more examples of simple elegance addressing other environmental issues:

✓ Pole-mounted solar collectors allow the ground underneath them to be used for agriculture

- ✓ Bicycles, bike trailers, pedicabs, and all the other variations on pedal-powered transport of people and goods

- ✓ Small-space "vertical gardens" let apartment-dwellers grow their own food in about one square meter/square yard

- ✓ The simple mesh nets we use to keep birds from devouring our berry crops—no pesticides needed or wanted

Simple innovations like these create huge market opportunities for pioneering green entrepreneurs.

Green Variations on Traditional **Business**

As the world gets smarter about the need to go green, millions of consumers are looking for greener ways of doing the things they've been doing all along. And smart businesses owners are right there with them, offering greener ways to do business and spreading their green attitude.

Here are a few among numerous examples of businesses that are successfully filling that green market niche.

Green Real Estate

More and more brokers are actively marketing green properties. A few have gone so far as to affiliate themselves with green real estate broker associations such as EcoBroker.com. The home page of EcoBroker triages visitors  into three channels: consumers who want to buy or sell a green home; brokers who'd like to get certified as green-aware; and vendors of green products and services who could benefit from an affiliate relationship—everything from green architects and builders to suppliers of renewable energy certificates.

(This section uses a fairly expensive paid-placement model, and as of this writing, most of the categories are empty—rather surprising for a website launched in 2004, and disconcerting for visitors. If I were EcoBroker, I'd either switch to free basic listings with payment for enhanced, or get rid of any categories that have no entries.)

Where the site does build trust is in the section on "Green Topics": numerous articles, some of them fairly technical, on various aspects of building, renovating, and living in a green home, or working in a green building.

Printing

Putting words onto paper has all sorts of environmental issues: logging forests, chemicals in the waste water, paper going into landfills after it's read, carbon impact of powering all those presses (to name a few).

However, you have lots of leeway to choose a printer who's working hard to minimize negative environmental impacts. Things to look for include

- ✓ Forest Stewardship Council or other reputable certification that monitors chain-of-custody from the time the wood is harvested until the paper is used (note: there are several different levels of FSC certification, so make sure you know what you're getting)

- ✓ Recycled paper, processed without chlorine bleach, with a high post-consumer waste (PCW) percentage

- ✓ Renewable energy used for all or most of the printing plant's energy needs (a net-zero building is even better)

- ✓ Short-run and on-demand printing options, allowing customers to use just-in-time inventory management instead of warehousing large quantities of printed materials.

- ✓ Recycling of paper-roll ends and other usable scrap

- ✓ Biodegradable, vegetable-based inks

- ✓ Zero contamination of water sources through waste discharge

Most printing companies offer at least a selection of recycled paper these days (and often at prices comparable to non-recycled). Some go much farther, incorporating many of the items in our checklist, above. And some actively market their green commitments; my eighth book, Guerrilla Marketing Goes Green, examines three different attempts by three different printers to make themselves attractive to green customers.

Lodging

As with printing, pretty much every hotel, inn, and B&B has adopted at least some green best practices—if nothing else, the relatively recent custom of not changing all the towels and linens every day.

But in this industry, too, the smart ones are doing much more—such as:

- ✓ Installing water-conserving showerheads, toilets, and faucet aerators

- ✓ Serving filtered water in reusable pitchers and glasses, instead of water bottles and disposable cups

✓ Generating power through solar, wind, hydro, etc.

✓ Incorporating local organic food into meal and snack choices—and accommodating greener diets such as vegetarian and vegan

✓ Composting food wastes, either on-site or by donating to local farmers

✓ Putting plantings and potted plants in public areas

✓ Setting no-smoking policies

And they're basing much of their marketing on these initiatives. Here, for instance, is a passage from the home page of a very environmentally aware B&B: "first solar-powered, off-the-grid, bed and breakfast [in the state]. Our B&B opened in 2008 so we could showcase the ease of solar-living, provide you with a 'green' getaway, and share our land, our animals and our farm. We are just 5 minutes from town, but light years from the noise, hustle, and hassle of city life."

How can you incorporate more green principles into a conventional business—and how can you then get the most marketing advantage from doing so?

d.light: Bringing **Sustainable Lighting** to Address Desperate Need

Perhaps you've read the game-shifting book The Fortune at the Bottom of the Pyramid, by C.K. Prahalad (you can read my review at www.principledprofit.com/subscribe-2#fortune). Arguing that the most economically disadvantaged people on the planet not only create a great market for those entrepreneurs brave enough to

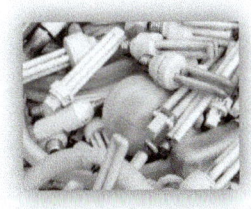

venture into that territory, but also that developing countries provide a terrific testing ground for innovation and cost control, Prahalad offers numerous examples of companies that are profiting handsomely while serving the poorest of the poor.

Here in the green world, we can look at that innovation potential through a lens of deep sustainability and multiple benefits. And the possibilities are awesome.

It's been a while since I've profiled a company in this space. This month, we take a look at one of those companies, simultaneously addressing poverty, education, air pollution/toxic fumes/health risks, energy savings, carbon footprint, and more—and making a huge difference in lives of those at the bottom of the economic pyramid. And the company does all this with a simple three-item product line.

d.light, headquartered in San Francisco and with additional offices in China, India, and Kenya, sells inexpensive freestanding bright-light LED lanterns with lifetime batteries powered by dual solar/plug-in electric chargers. The company's mission statement: "to create new freedoms for customers without access to reliable power so they can enjoy a brighter future."

And to accomplish this mission, the company employs a deeply holistic analysis of the problems faced by people at the bottom of the heap, and how a reliable and renewable source of good light can help solve them.

The lights go into two types of environments: places where light has been supplied by kerosene (or, conceivably, open fires)—and those with no pre-existing night-time light source.

If the lantern replaces an existing kerosene model, it accomplishes many desirable goals: providing a better quality of light that needs no fuel, does not produce toxic fumes, has no risk of setting the house on fire, reduces  pollution, and leaves considerably more money in the hands of the family using the lantern—because the savings over purchasing kerosene typically pays for the lantern in about two months.

Where the lantern provides light in a previously unlit area, the benefits are different, but just as significant: four more hours per day of productive time. Children can advance much farther with their studies; cottage industries, farms, and microbusinesses can produce and sell more. In short, the lamp becomes a ladder out of poverty.

Using classic Prahalad-inspired design principles, the units are cheap, extremely durable, and designed for multiple environments. A company video shows the lamps dropped from a high balcony and run over by a car, and still working afterward. At least one of the three models can be mounted on a wall or ceiling. The top-line model can also charge mobile phones. In developing countries, payment plans can be arranged for less than the previous cost of kerosene; in developed countries, 10 percent of the proceeds goes to fund lamps for children who could not buy them. Worldwide, they're sold with a two-year free-replacement warranty.

And the company, currently operating 6000 retail outlets in 40 countries, is very successful, both financially and in the social and environmental good it has created. As of February 28, 2013, the company claims:

- ✓ 13,638,438 "lives empowered" [that is, units sold]

- ✓ 3,409,610 school-aged children reached with solar lighting

- ✓ $275,817,462 saved in energy-related expenses

- ✓ 3,589,490,280 productive hours created for working and studying

- ✓ 656,952 tons of CO_2 offset

- ✓ 10,115,224 kWh generated from renewable energy source

(You can find the latest update of these statistics at www.dlightdesign.com/impact-dashboard/).

These stats, as I confirmed by e-mail discussion with company spokesperson Darin Kingston of the India office, were arrived at by looking at the maximum possible utilization for each category—and that means they may be overstating the benefits somewhat.

I asked Darin if he was double-counting—wasn't it true that if you max out the possible benefit, you can have either the $275 million in energy savings and the 657-ton CO_2 offset (replacing kerosene) OR the 3.6 billion newly productive hours (replacing darkness), but not both at once? But he assured me that no, they're not double-counting; the productivity benefit stems from the longer number of hours and better quality of light compared to kerosene. He did acknowledge that the stats assume a one-to-one relationship between the new lanterns and the kerosene lamps they replace.

Company executives hope to grow that user base from 13 million all the way to 100 million by the end of the decade—perhaps not an unrealistic estimate considering the company was only conceived of in 2004, following founder Sam Goldman's encounter as a Peace Corps volunteer in Africa with a neighbor child who had been badly burned in a kerosene spill.

It's good to see a company doing well by doing so much good—and combining environmental, social, and health benefits to serve the most needy.

Nature's Business Model:
100 Percent Recycling, Zero Energy Consumption

Recycling, as we usually think of it, is a huge step forward compared to letting materials rot (or worse, not rot, ever) in a landfill. But recycling, the way it typically works, has its own issues. Conventional recycling requires massive inputs of energy to convert our trash into something not-quite-as-usable as the original material.

So, for instance, high-quality petroleum-based PET is good enough to store beverages for human consumption. When mingled with other plastics and processed at a recycling plant, it's good enough to make "cloth" for shopping bags, or planks for decking and park benches. But it's no longer good enough to store things that people will drink.

Now the good news: the world gives us many better models than this. In biology, things work differently. Every biological element breaks up (I am deliberately not saying "breaks down") into an input for something else—starting with the basic lifecycle: animals convert oxygen into carbon dioxide, the breath-of-life for plants—and plants convert the CO_2 to our breath-of-life: oxygen. How cool is that?

Similarly, think of how compost works. A tree branch falls in the woods—or a family gathers their organic wastes in a bin outside. Various insects, mammals, birds, and fungi begin to digest it. And eventually, miraculously, it turns into a brand new product: fresh, nutrient-rich soil.

And both the breath cycle and the compost cycle (among many other examples in nature) do their amazing work with zero waste, and with zero need for human-produced energy.

Humans can look at how nature works and come up with fresh, creative, dare-I-say brilliant new processes to do what nature does, and to do it without consuming energy. The trick is to look at what can use any particular waste product as a new input for a new process.

I've known about this for quite a few years, and have several examples of this thinking in my eighth book, Guerrilla Marketing Goes Green. Here, for instance, is an excerpt from the book, discussing the amazing work of an entrepreneur named John Todd:

In downtown Burlington and South Burlington, Vermont, you'll find a very unusual industrial park: a place where brewery wastes turn into a growing environment for mushrooms—and in the process create an enjoyable biopark, a green and vibrant ecosystem in the middle of the business district, where downtown workers can enjoy a unique natural setting.

Welcome to the Intervale, 700 acres of sustainable enterprises and ecofriendly public spaces.

Todd, like other visionaries I profile in the book, is an entrepreneur. He is making money leveraging nature's principles to remedy major issues such as pollution and rampant disease—both human-caused and nature caused. He's using biological principles to clean up stagnant lakes, to purify water in developing countries where safe water is a rarity.

Not that it's always simple. Listen to Todd explain what he did to clean up a lagoon that had been choking on the waste from a chicken processing plant:

"We planted restorers with 28,000 different species of higher plants and animals. It grew very quickly. Each was designed to break down or sequester different compounds. We reduced the electrical power to convert the waste by 80 percent and cut capital costs in half."

One of the underlying principles in this work is sharing resources among different pieces of the system and changing the paradigm about what's left over. Instead of disposing of a waste stream, Todd encourages people to think about how to use that material as an input. The goal is zero emissions: no waste generation at all. If wastes are considered as inputs, they can lead to new commercial enterprises—for instance, a mushroom farm. All of a sudden, the cost of waste disposal turns into capital for a new revenue stream.

This is how the natural world works, at least when undisturbed by human pollution. When these systems are integrated together, they not only eliminate waste, but also provide shared synergy, reduce costs, spread technical and legal expertise, and create both economic and environmental improvements—as occurred at the Intervale, where biowastes feed a commercial fish farm that also cleans the water, and the waste heat from a wood-fired power plant is recaptured to heat the complex.

But the real lesson is this: every problem is an economic opportunity for a visionary entrepreneur. And those who can solve the world's problems with zero waste, high-quality outputs, and zero grid-based or human-produced energy are on track for success.

Will YOU be the next to create a business like this?

(Note: This article was inspired by the article, "A 'Circular Economy': Why the Next Packaging Will Be Grown, Not Manufactured," on Good: http://www.good.is/posts/mushrooms-based-packaging-and-designing-a-circular-economy

Educate Your Customers to Do an Easy **"Green Reboot"**

As a business owner or manager, or as someone who works in a nonprofit or government agency, you probably have more influence than you think. Why not use that influence to both help your customers go green in ways they may not have thought about AND establish yourself even more firmly in their minds as a green organization that cares about the world. Forward-thinking companies around the world have been doing this for years—why not you?

Every point of interaction is a chance to educate your public: product packaging, in-store signage, advertisements, social media messaging, press coverage, a bulletin board in the reception area, the home page of your website and Facebook page, email and printed newsletters, brochures, and more—all opportunities to do good in the world by talking about the green steps you take, and the green steps your readers, viewers, listeners, and customers can take.

What sorts of messages can you promote?

Of course, you want to discuss the green steps your organization has taken or will take shortly: the motivation for the change, the impact it has, the way it changes what is possible.

But why stop there? Use this "bully pulpit" to educate and inform a captive audience about why and how THEY should go green.

The how is as important as the why; lots of people are philosophically inclined to go green but have never really thought about the easy ways they can go greener in their personal lives.

And much of that lack is because of bad training—so you can make a difference by helping people retrain. It makes even better sense if you pick aspects of green behavior that relate directly to your own mission. Here are some examples:

We are trained to turn the faucet on full blast and leave it spewing precious water the whole time we wash a dish or brush our teeth. Educate your customers to turn on a small stream of water during the actual washing and rinsing, and to turn it completely off for the between part while they scrub or brush. Dentists, dish soap companies, sponge and kitchen appliance manufacturers or retailers: this is an opportunity for you. Run a restaurant? Post water-saving tips in your restroom or place them on a table tent.

We are trained to pull off a huge wad of toilet paper every time, most of which is completely wasted. Educate your customers at how effectively they can wipe with just a few squares—especially if you make or distribute paper products, or bathroom fixtures.

We are trained to fill up a whole kettle every time we want just one cup of tea, then to either pour the extra down the drain—behavior that borders on criminal, if you ask me—or waste energy to reboil the same water again, sometimes several times. Florists and garden supply stores, why not suggest that your customers water the plants with the surplus water, once it's cool? Plate and cutlery companies can recommend soaking dishes with the extra. Tea and energy companies can point out that the tea is better tasting if it's not reboiled, but in a way that discourages the down-the-drain "solution." Kettle makers can run contests for the best ways to recycle the extra water left in the kettle.

We are trained to jump in a car, by ourselves, and drive even very short distances. Ridesharing companies can encourage carpooling; bicycle and mass transit companies as well as healthcare providers can demonstrate the benefits of not driving at all.

Need more ideas about your opportunities to connect with your customers and change their behavior? Here in New England, there's a famous old slogan that can help you discover the possibilities: "Use it up, wear it out, make it do, or do without."

One resource that can help educate your customers is an e-book I've written called *Painless Green: 111 Tips to Help the Environment, Lower Your Carbon Footprint, Cut Your Budget, and Improve Your Quality of Life-With No Negative Impact on Your Lifestyle.* Contact me if you'd like to use this resource in your educational efforts.

How is the **Green Economy Saving Money** in Your Business?

You often hear that going green is too expensive. Answer those critics with the ways going green is actually cheaper than staying brown. And there are many of those "low-hanging fruit" savings areas. So you can put those into place in your own business, start saving money to fund more expensive green improvements, and gain some bragging rights in your marketing.

What are we talking about? Here are two among dozens of possibilities.

Switching to LEDs

Switching out any remaining incandescent light bulbs for LEDs (you can skip CFLs, which are not as efficient as LEDs and have waste disposal issues because they contain mercury). Using the savings calculator at http://www.ledwaves.com/led-calc.html

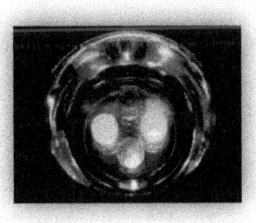

shows just how much you can save. Let's say you run a retail store. If you replace 50 100-watt, 1000-hour lifespan bulbs that cost you $1 each with 10-watt, 50,000-hour bulbs that cost $10 each, over the life of the bulbs, you get to bank an extra $24,991.00—based on operating 10 hours a day at a relatively low commercial electricity rate of 10 cents per kilowatt hour. You break even less than three months after switching the bulbs.

Not bad—but now let's say you run a high-ceilinged location like a basketball court. You replace the same 50 bulbs, but you also have to pay a worker to go out in a cherry picker every time you change a bulb. How much does the labor, fuel, and depreciation/maintenance cost you? $50? $100? More? Let's be generous to the nongreens and say it's $50, and furthermore, we'll say your worker replaces an average of three bulbs every time, rather than just one, so the net cost per bulb is $16.70 for the labor and vehicle use, plus another buck for the replacement incandescent bulb. Thus each new incandescent bulb is going to cost $17.70 to purchase and install.

The calculator informs us that you eliminated 2500 bulb changes by switching to LEDs, and you won't have to change them again for 13 years. If I'm figuring this correctly, multiplying $17.70 times 2500 saves an astonishing $4,425,000.

Changing Your Printing and Copying Habits

Here's an example more relevant to smaller entrepreneurs, including home-based businesses like my own. Six years ago, when my laser printer wore out, I replaced it with a duplexing printer— one that's designed to print on both sides. I also  changed my default setting to duplex printing (Note: I don't advise feeding used paper back into a single-sided printer; you might encounter problems like toner getting sucked into the rollers.)

Just this simple change dropped my paper bill by about 40 percent (not 50 percent, because some print jobs are an odd number of pages). The savings added up quickly because I use recycled paper that costs about $40 or $50 per case.

I also bumped up the font size for screen viewing—another simple change that saved oodles of paper. I used to print documents as short as five pages because it was fatiguing to read them onscreen. But by setting the View mode to 125 or 150 percent, I can usually read 20 or 25 pages comfortably.

And I got in the habit of using Print Preview. Often, especially when printing from the Web, I see that I don't need to print several pages at the end. In Word documents, I often find a single blank page at the end, and delete before printing.

In short, by thinking strategically about printing, you can lower your costs and your carbon footprint. Similarly, before copying, think about who really needs to see the document, and whether it makes more sense to send it electronically rather than run off a bunch of copies.

I'd love to hear what you're doing to save money while greening your own business. Please write to me at shel AT greenandprofitable.com with the subject line, "**How I'm Greening My Business Affordably**" (you might even get publicity in a future column).

Biofuels: **Good and Bad** Models to **Learn From**

Those of us who want a greener world can learn a lot from the biofuel industry. Both positive and negative lessons abound.

The first and perhaps most important lesson is to think things through. What appears on the surface to be a wonderful solution may not be so wonderful after all. In the case of biofuels, a lot of the technologies turned out to be full of unintended consequences.

Two technologies have been particularly troubling: corn ethanol and burning biomass. Both have turned out to be expensive, polluting, high-carbon-footprint, and resource-consuming. And both have diverted both land and what grows on the land from their highest potential uses.

Corn ethanol takes prime farmland out of food production and diverts it to energy. Wood-burning biomass plants lead to forest destruction. Neither is clean, and with corn ethanol, the ratio of energy consumed to energy generated is far from pretty. Both worsen the potential for harmful climate change, and both can lead to problems including monocropping, drastically reduced biodiversity and wildlife habit, and even higher food prices.

But should we write off biofuels altogether? Not at all.

Many much more promising technologies can actually reduce pollution and generate energy without interfering with food production or habitat. For instance:

The farm I live on is currently installing a methane digester that will actually remove greenhouse gasses while providing enough electricity to power 250 homes. Its inputs? Cow manure and food waste!

In Brazil, sugarcane waste underpins a vast ethanol industry, strengthened by a government requirement to mix ethanol with gasoline (and government incentives to produce ethanol), all the way back to 1976. As a result, almost the entire Brazilian vehicle fleet runs either on flex-fuel mixtures of ethanol and gasoline, or on pure ethanol.
(More information: en.wikipedia.org/wiki/Ethanol_fuel_in_Brazil)

In the United States, where I live, many companies are successfully harvesting waste frying oil from fast-food restaurants and converting the waste oil to biodiesel. One particularly spiffy model is Green Circle North Carolina, which adds some beautiful new pieces to create a circle of community self-sufficiency: donating a portion of the profits to the schools, offering restaurants the PR benefits of supporting local school districts, and then selling the biodiesel to those school districts to power their school buses. When we as green entrepreneurs create these sorts of win-win-win programs, the whole world benefits.

There have also been many successful experiments generating ethanol with nonfood crops that can grow on marginal land, such as switchgrass. These have tended to yield more energy and create fewer greenhouse gases. (More information: www.scientificamerican.com/article.cfm?id=grass-makes-better-ethanol-than-corn). And then there's the so-called Q Microbe, that its backers claim will digest far more cellulose and produce much more energy from the same amount of biomass. However, commercializing the Q Microbe, first identified by researchers at the University of Massachusetts several years ago, has been off to a very rocky start. Qteros (the company that has tried to bring this technology to market) has faced many funding and operational challenges—including changes in ownership and having to close its plant—and its future is unclear.

From my perspective, the more successful and promising technologies have something in common: they create energy out of what we're accustomed to thinking of as waste: materials that would

 have either clogged up landfills or emitted greenhouse gases when incinerated. Furthermore, they are not the food parts of food crops; they're either waste parts of food plants, or plants that are not used for food (and aren't grown on prime agricultural land).

In other words, they are part of a holistic approach to thinking about the integration of our energy and food systems, and not a poorly-thought-out kludge grafted onto a system not designed to accommodate it, all too often with disastrous consequences.

In one sense, biofuel is our oldest energy source. When aboriginal societies first discovered, thousands of years ago, that fire could not only keep them warm on cold winter nights but could preserve food while making it both easier to digest and better tasting, they were burning wood and plant matter. Back then, of course, they didn't worry about greenhouse gas emissions.

In short, as with wind, solar, and hydro, we can find both right and wrong ways to develop new energy sources. In tomorrow's world, sensible biofuel will be part of the mix.

What I **Learned** from my **Energy Audit**

January was much colder than usual here—and my old farmhouse (built in 1743) was feeling unusually chilly—especially the kitchen, which we'd just redone.

It had been a few years since our last energy audit, so I set one up.

The first thing I learned was why my house has felt so much colder this year. The house had been insulated by the previous owner, probably in the 1970s. And the insulation was fiberglass, which has a definite lifespan. We'd been told the last time we'd had an audit that the insulation was aging; this time, we were told it was past its usefulness.

But beyond the worn-out fiberglass (not the most ecological material to begin with)—the whole house was leaking air all over the place. As I walked around the house with the auditor, he pointed out chinks in the basement foundation, spaces between beams and walls, beams and ceilings, and walls and ceilings, gaps between the wooden pieces of our skylights.

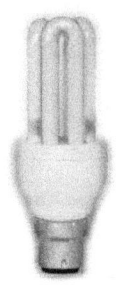

And we finally found out why the kitchen was even colder than the rest of the house: our new energy-saving LED light fixtures, ironically enough, were not insulated and tapped into the very coldest part of the house: a second-floor kneewall running the length of the longest side. The quality of light and the amazingly low energy consumption of the lights is fabulous—but who knew it would have such an impact on our home heating?

No wonder we've had to turn the thermostat higher lately!

The auditor suggested we could fix the LED air infiltration problem with spray-foam insulation. However, in that room, where we just spent a large amount of money to redo it, aesthetics are a big consideration. When I applied some of that foam in another part of the house, I found it very hard to control, and the results were less-than-pretty. So I think we'll wait until we can find someone to do it who can make it look nice.

The vendor for the energy audit outlined several steps we could do to alleviate the situation—each of which cost about double what I would have expected to pay. If we did everything he told us to, we'd have been looking at well over $18,000. Even if it saved us as much as $500 per year—highly unlikely, considering that's about 25 percent of an entire heating bill—that's a 36-year payback. Not a very good return on investment, even for a green guy like me.

Fortunately, since he had walked me around the house and shown me the areas where cold air was infiltrating, I could fix the most glaring problems myself, with rope caulk or spray-foam insulation. I am doing this a little at a time, and already notice huge improvement in the room where I've been concentrating: my grown daughter's former bedroom, which is where I keep my exercise bike. Just by caulking the skylight and foaming some of the air spaces, I'm able to use a lot less electric heat in that room. It doesn't get nearly as cold, and when I preheat the room before an exercise session, I can come back in a lot faster. In short, the savings are immediate.

Over the next few weeks, I'll be sealing up a lot of these cracks all around the house. I'm expecting a substantial reduction of energy use and much greater comfort as I work my way through the project. Cost? About $20 US, and some short periods of time when I need a break from the computer anyway.

Also fortunately, we live in an area where many vendors are competing in the insulation arena. So we'll get a few more estimates, and find a vendor who can deliver value as well as comfort.

Lessons and Takeaways

So what did we learn from this experience?

- ✓ Even a building that was well-insulated in its day may need some refreshing after some years.

- ✓ Look at value received over money spent. Do the little, inexpensive things ithat have a big impact to get a measurable result.

- ✓ Don't accept the first estimate you receive; check a few competitors.

Postscript: We had a different vendor come in to do an energy audit a few months later, through our utility company. Because the utility is under pressure to reduce demand, it actually funds not only the audit, but much of the work. During the audit, nearly all our remaining non-LED light bulbs, our showerheads, our thermostat, and a couple of our power strips were all replaced at no cost to us.

Following the audit, we contracted with the firm to implement most of the recommendations. The end result: for a few hundred dollars out of pocket, we got extensive insulation and a much warmer, more comfortable house with a far lower fuel consumption—and even counting the utility's contribution, a total cost of about 1/9 the first vendor's estimate.

* * *

I enjoyed writing this column from 2010 to 2014, and I think I provided very high value for those who read it. Unfortunately, I never got enough markets to make the project economically viable.

As I move in the direction of helping companies see the value in solving problems like hunger, poverty, war, and climate catastrophe, I can no longer afford the luxury of doing this column for the few markets that subscribed. So this will be the last issue for a while.

I'd love to bring it back, if I can get to a minimum number of subscribers each paying just $10 per month. If you have possible markets for me, please drop me a line at shel AT greenandprofitable.com with the subject "Column Market."

Disclaimer: The very observant among you may notice that some examples come up more than once. Keep in mind that this ebook is a compilation of a monthly column that ran for four years. I have organized the columns by topic rather than chronologically here, and as a result, columns that may have been years apart end up close to each other in the same ebook. Yes, some examples are repeated, but they were inserted to make different points, at different times. Please also note that nothing in this ebook series should be taken as legal or professional advice, and as in any situation, your results may vary as you implement the tips and ideas.

About Shel Horowitz and
Business For a Better World

Green business profitability expert Shel Horowitz shows businesses how to profit both by going green and by addressing problems like hunger and poverty, war, violence, and catastrophic climate change. Active in both marketing and the environment since his teen years in the early 1970s, Shel is the award-winning author of eight books including long-running Amazon category bestseller *Guerrilla Marketing Goes Green*.

- ✓ As a consultant, Shel brings laser focus to turning problems into opportunities, opening new markets, and helping you identify potential partners.

- ✓ As a marketing and informational copywriter trained in journalism, Shel is known for his clear writing, ability to make technical concepts accessible, and his skill in telling "the story behind the story" to move people to action.

- ✓ As an international speaker and trainer, Shel combines dynamic vocal style with powerful graphics and gets his audiences actively involved. He's spoken at major business and environmental conferences in locations as diverse as Istanbul, Davos (Switzerland), and Honolulu.

After over a decade actively assisting green businesses with their marketing, Shel branched out in 2014 to help businesses seize profit opportunities in turning hunger and poverty into sufficiency, war and violence into peace, and catastrophic climate change into planetary balance—and helping individuals reclaim their power to actively create this better world.

Shel is happy to talk to you about helping in any of these areas. Reach him at 413-586-2388 (8 a.m. to 10 p.m. US Eastern Time), email shel AT greenandprofitable.com, or find him on Twitter @ShelHorowitz.

Shel also has a gift for you: a free copy of his ebook, *Painless Green: 111 Tips to Help the Environment, Lower Your Carbon Footprint, Cut Your Budget, and Improve Your Quality of Life—With No Negative Impact on Your Lifestyle*. To claim your free copy of this $9.95 ebook, visit PainlessGreenBook.com/earthday and use the code, G&Pebook.

One more set of gifts, FREE with your no-cost subscription to Shel Horowitz's monthly Clean and Green Newsletter:

- ✓ Seven Tips to Gain Marketing Traction as a Green Guerrilla

- ✓ Seven Weeks to a Greener Business: once a week for seven weeks, tips on going greener with printing, energy saving, waste reduction, water conservation, transportation, going deep-green, and of course, green marketing.

- ✓ Plus the informative monthly newsletter, published since 1997 and featuring a business tip or profile plus a book review each issue.

Sign up in the upper-right-hand corner at http://greenandprofitable.com.

Green and
Profitable

BOOK 2

**Marketing
Strategy/Messages
For Green Businesses**

Shel Horowitz

Raising the Bar on **Green Marketing**

The old green messages are beginning to look a bit pale. Accusations of greenwashing are rife, and often, those charges have more than a little substance—does anyone really believe BP is a green company anymore?

So does that mean green marketing is dead? What's a conscious marketer to do?

First of all, I don't for a moment believe that green is dying, let alone dead. But just as parents stop diapering their babies once they've been toilet trained and expect them to wipe their own tushes from that point on, so we as green marketers need to take greater responsibility for our messaging. Like those toddlers who are mastering not only toilet training but walking and talking and table manners and a whole bunch of other stuff all at once, we have to stand on our own feet, even if it feels a bit wobbly at first.

So here are a few marketing guideposts on your own wobble toward sustainable marketing:

1) Be clear and specific. Today's informed consumer doesn't just want to hear "we've gone green." They'll respond better to something like "by introducing this new,

efficient packing machine, we've reduced solid waste by 18 percent and cut carbon emissions by 368 tons a year."

2) Make consumers understand what each of these accomplishments means to them: "That solid waste reduction means we don't have to bring nearly as much to the landfill, which means lower costs passed on to you, longer landfill life, and fewer non-degradable materials clogging up the landfill. Lower carbon means 68 fewer asthma cases in our county every year, as well as reducing catastrophic global warming."

3) If you're familiar with the concept of features vs. benefits, you'll note that the first bullet stresses features—which are by themselves seldom enough to sell successfully—and the second bullet translates those features into direct benefits both to the consumer and to the world. Features let the gear-heads (who already understand what they mean) supply the benefits themselves); benefits speak to average consumers through their own emotional needs and wants, and are much more powerful. In many cases, you need both.

4) Raise the bar on your industry's standards for going green. Have you achieved zero waste in a facet of production? Have you not just switched to compostable plastics but actually begun to compost them? Have you figured out a way to cut energy or water use by some huge percentage? Are you sourcing a larger percentage of materials from sustainable-practices vendors? Say so! You'll get the competitive advantage of doing this before others—and once your competitors start imitating, you can still get good marketing mileage out of having been first.

Stay away from messaging that won't be believed. If you're promoting nuclear power or large-scale biomass, for example, any attempt to portray your company as green will come back to bite you. Best, of course, is not to promote those products at all, but if you have to promote them, get out of the green space and find other ways to market (or should I say, defend) these environmentally toxic technologies. Both of these have been promoted as green alternatives, and neither one passes the sniff test.

If the green content of your practices is questionable or largely unknown, be prepared to document it in your messaging—thoroughly.

I went to a solar festival where a couple of the exhibitors were talking about "biochar." From their materials, it looked to me like just another variant on burning wood: points for renewability, certainly, but NOT for clean emissions or carbon impact reduction.

By failing to convince me that they were truly green, these companies left me highly skeptical of other claims they (or their competitors) might make.

As I learned more about biochar over the next few years, I became convinced that there actually is merit in the green argument for biochar. But these first vendors I encountered didn't make a strong enough case.

Involve your supply chain. Just as "no man is an island," neither is a corporation. You have vendors who sell to you, and customers who buy from you. You have ancillary services involved, such as transportation or security. And you have both carrot- and stick-flavored leverage you can exert to help these companies go green. The carrots: not only will they get more of your business, but you will promote them in your green marketing campaigns. The stick? If they fail your sustainability criteria, you'll choose another vendor who is more earth-centered.

Don't Hide Your **Light**!

The box says "100% of the electricity used to manufacture these crackers and this container come from green power sources," and has a nice little accompanying graphic of a windmill. Just above this is a Forest Stewardship Council certification logo denoting sustainably harvested timber sources for the box.

This is a company that's doing the right thing, right?

Wrong. Both of these logos and statements are on the bottom panel of the box, where no one can see it unless they've already bought the crackers—or perhaps if the prospect accidentally knocks the package off the supermarket shelf, happens to land the bottom facing up, and somehow notices the small logos while picking up the box.

In other words, the marketing benefit of their commitment is just slightly above zero.

This particular package has plenty of white space on the front panel, prime real estate that does have a heksher (Kosher certification logo) but otherwise, does very little marketing at all.

This cracker company (which I will not name publicly) is far from alone.

Another example, which I highlight as a case study in my talks, is the household paper products company, Marcal. When I ask my audiences what year they think Marcal switched to recycled paper, most of the answers tend to fall between 1985 and 2005. Occasionally someone will guess a year in the 1970s, especially if I call the company a pioneer in using recycled stock.

Not once has anyone guessed the correct answer—1950—or even the correct decade. Because, for too long, like the cracker company, Marcal kept its best marketing point hidden. Even though the company has been 100% recycled for more than 60 years, it was only in the  past decade that it started incorporating this vital message into its packaging—and only since 2009 that environmental branding has become the central focus of its message to consumers.

You just have to wonder how much more toilet paper, napkins, tissues and paper towels the company would have sold if it had started bragging earlier. I know that when I first became aware of environmental concerns in the early 1970s, I would have been thrilled to find a cost-competitive brand that was also very green.

Like Marcal, the Swiss cereal company Familia has been using sustainable practices—in this case, buying grains from sustainable farms—for decades. But it was only early in 2010 that I noticed this was finally explained on its packaging.

These are three examples among hundreds.

Why do companies take the time and trouble to do good in the world, and then act like they're embarrassed about it? Perhaps it's a matter of corporate humility, not wanting to brag. In some cases, maybe it's worry about being accused of greenwashing—an accusation that could definitely hurt.

In Marcal's case, it may have started as a legitimate fear that people wouldn't buy household paper made of other people's castoffs, even if it was just their sterilized junkmail. In the conformist, status-conscious 1950s, it may not have been seen as a marketing strength, but as a liability.

But certainly by 1980 if not well before, what we now call Cultural Creatives were a well-established and rapidly growing marketing demographic. As far back as the 2000 publication of their book, _The Cultural Creatives: How 50 Million People Are Changing the World_, Paul H. Ray and Sherry Ruth Anderson estimated that more than a quarter of all adults in the developed countries they studied fell into this category. A quarter of the population!

Greenwashing accusations are easily defused with one simple rule: tell the truth. As for corporate humility, it's not doing those companies any favors.

I see both a bottom-line advantage and a save-the-world benefit to trumpeting an honest green message. On the financial side, you're able to market much more effectively to that vast market segment.

But even more to the point, you help make the world a better place. Every time a company shares its green initiatives publicly, it shows consumers that there are sustainable alternatives, pressures competitors to also go green, and continues to generate momentum toward a better world.

The Secret of Building a
New Market Lies within these
Five Simple Questions

If you've been struggling to build a green business, or to offer green products or services through an existing business, this column might just make your day—because I'm going to share the single biggest component of determining whether you will have a viable market for your offering.

All you have to do is ask yourself five simple questions:

1) What problem can you solve, or desire can you facilitate?

2) How is your method different from and better than existing solutions (what are the advantages, in other words)?

3) Who needs this problem solved strongly enough that they're willing to pay (who is the market)?

4) How do you reach those people?

5) How do you convince them to buy?

Let's see how this works out with a case study—an actual example I ran into recently.

Problem/Desire:

Thousands of gallons of water per household are wasted flushing small amounts of urine. An entrepreneur would like to help people save this water.

Possible Solutions:

There are several possible ways to fix this, such as composting toilets, graywater recycling (so that the water for flushing has already been used once, in a sink, dishwasher, shower, bath, or washing machine), and European-style two-way toilet switches that allow you to select a large flow for solids or a smaller flow for liquids. But this particular entrepreneur chose a different route: Go Flushless, an enzyme compound that elimates the odor and stain, allowing the urine to remain in the bowl with no ill effects.

Advantages:

Most of the other solutions involve extensive hardware modifications, and that's expensive. Go Flushless, by comparison, is cheap to buy and easy to implement (a couple of squirts on a standard hand-operated spray pump such as you'd use for window cleaner).

Possible Markets:

Green consumers who care about saving water are an obvious market—and because of the low point of entry, the product appeals not only to homeowners but also to renters. But there are several other markets, too.

Large consumers of water have economic reasons to save. Think about how much water is consumed in the bathrooms of sports stadiums, concert halls, schools, transportation terminals, and so forth. However, to reach this market, there would have to be a way to control the flush schedule remotely, which might be difficult in most circumstances (other than public urinals, some of which already use a timer instead of individual flush handles). So this would be a back-burner market, to pursue later once the technology catches up or the social expectations around flushing have shifted enough to create a space in the market within the society as a whole.

But there's another huge market that's much easier to reach: homeowners who live with septic systems and private water supplies (their own or a neighborhood well). Unlike the owners of large public bathrooms, this group has no technological or sociological challenges in  implementing the Go Flushless method, and has a strong interest in conserving water so as to extend the lifespan of its infrastructure while decreasing the number of septic tank pumpouts.

Finally, there is another large market: people who live in places that face drought frequently, and where the culture has shifted in favor of flushing less—as it has in California, for example. Those folks are already letting the yellow stuff sit, and they would welcome a simple solution to the problem of odors and stains.

How to Reach these Markets:

These four different markets are going to congregate in different places.

For green consumers, exhibiting at a green festival makes a lot of sense. In fact, I met company owners Bill and Jane Monetti at a green festival where I was speaking and they were exhibiting—and selling quite a bit of their product.

Articles in trade magazines would effectively reach the industrial users. Homeowners with septic systems might best be reached through direct mail or even in-person sales calls. And people in drought-centric cultures could be reached simply enough by mass-market media such as radio, TV, and print newspapers.

And of course, although the message points would be different, it's important to note that the marketing techniques can transcend the barriers and reach every group. With different audience-specific messages, the Monettis could actively use social media, blogs, traditional media publicity, public speaking, product demonstrations, and their own website (no name a few examples).

Getting the Sale:

Target your appeals to each of these audiences. For green homeowners and tenants, saving water is enough of a reason. For the industrial bathroom owners as well as the well and septic crowd, a purely economic argument is going to work. And for those already not flushing because of drought, an appeal based on a clean, germ-free house and a toilet that is once again easy to clean should close the sale.

CISA: Matching **Locavores** and **Local Farms**

In the Pioneer Valley of Massachusetts (where I happen to live), you'll find a whole lot of farms with signage calling them "Local Heroes." You'll also see similar signs in grocery stores, supermarkets, farmers markets, plant nurseries, and even cafes and restaurants. And you'll see bumper stickers all over the region that say, "Be a Local Hero, Buy Locally Grown®."

Where did these signs come from, and what do they mean?

They came from an organization called Community Involved in Sustaining Agriculture, or CISA. And they signify that these farms are active partners in the local economy. People who want local foods seek them out, and buy from them. And these farms willingly sell to a market that cuts out several of the middlemen and allows them to

command a premium price. In an era when farms are facing huge challenges economically, the CISA member farms tend to be doing well.

Consumers get fresh foods (often picked that day)—and the knowledge that they're building the *local* economy. The money they spend with these farmers and their retailers comes back to the community in a myriad of ways: from support for sports teams and community causes to preserving open space for farmland as urban sprawl tries to encroach.

And farmers get ready markets—both wholesale and retail—of locals committed to the local economy, and of stores or food service establishments willing to facilitate that commitment by making the products available. Interestingly, some of the stores and restaurants that participate are not themselves locally based; a couple of very large chains are participating, selling local produce to local buyers even while they themselves are headquartered far away.

CISA was founded in 1993 as the Pioneer Valley Alliance for Sustainable Agriculture, and rebranded as an incorporated charitable organization in 1999, under its current name. Local Hero launched the same year. It offers many support resources and programs to local farmers, in addition to the Local Hero campaign: a farm share program for elders...market development among large institutions such as schools and hospitals...filling infrastructure needs such as processing centers...technical assistance to new farmers...workshops and instructional materials on marketing, grant writing, organic farming, and more...financing options...

But its public face is very much associated with the wildly popular Local Hero program. And through that program, a lot of dollars have shifted to local sources. In fact, according to Devon Whitney-Deal, CISA's Local Hero

Member Services Coordinator and one of nine employees, when the organization started tracking in 2003, there were only nine farmers markets in the Pioneer Valley—but now there are at least 40 seasonal markets plus four winter markets (a more than 400 percent increase in eight years). CISA has 199 member farmers, 50 retailers, 32 restaurants, and a total membership of 312. And in its three-county service area, reversing the farm-loss trend elsewhere, more acreage is actually in farmland now than when the group was founded.

In other words, through a massive branding campaign, this organization actually *created a consciousness about buying local.* People who in the past had not thought much about where their food comes from have made a conscious shift to buying some portion of their food supply from local sources—and that, in turn, has helped the farm economy to stay solvent.

The buy-local strategy, according to CISA's website, offers these five benefits (quoting):

✓ Keeps money in the local economy

✓ Preserves family farms

✓ Reduces oil-dependent transportation costs

✓ Protects our local landscapes

✓ Ensures that fresh, healthy food stays available and affordable to all

You won't find CISA on the web at cisa.com, .org, or .net; you have to look at buylocalfood.org/ (and what a great URL). I'm rather surprised that the organization hasn't started a franchise-like model on the website, like Craig's List. You'd kind of expect that by now there might be, for example, sydney.buylocalfood.org or kualalumpur.buylocalfood.org.

Whether the program uses a franchise model or not, I would think many communities around the world would be eagerly replicating this very successful program.

The **Certification** Conundrum

Everyone knows that third-party endorsement is a powerful credibility builder. This is especially true in the green movement, where so much of the marketing process is based on making a strong case that you have other values besides financial gain.

Certification is one way to gain that credibility. When an independent agency verifies that you are doing what you say you're doing, customer trust of you and your products go way up.

But certification raises a number of other issues:

What Does the Claim Actually Mean?

In the green marketplace, numerous products make all sorts of claims. The purchaser has to sort out what's really going on, and which claims are meaningful. Smart shoppers understand, for instance, that when a package says, "made with organic ingredients," that means as much as 30 percent of the product could be nonorganic. They don't yet have enough information to make an educated choice. What percentage of the ingredients are organic? Which ingredients were grown that way? The pesticide content of a nonfood product like nonorganic cotton will likely be much higher than the pesticide content of a fruit with edible skin, such as apples; all of this has to be factored into the buying decision. So this particular group will turn over the box and look at the ingredients list and look at which ingredients are really organic, and in what order the organic and nonorganic ingredients appear (thus, their relative predominance).

Self-Labeling Versus True Certification

Many labels claim a product is "natural" or "fairly traded"—but no standards exist for what is natural or fairly traded, and no certifying body regulates the claims. Consumers are at the mercy of the manufacturer and have to hope for honesty. By contrast, the word "organic" has a legal definition, and a neutral-party certification such as USDA Organic in the United States or Ecocert for European cosmetics gives it teeth. And various agencies such as the 26 members around the world of Fairtrade International (from Australia to the US) certify compliance with fair trade provisions: If you see those types of certifications, you know the claim was independently verified.

Retailers are also stepping into the breach. Whole Foods, for instance, now requires certification for any product claiming to be organic.

Of course in today's wired world, shoppers themselves can play a role in verifying claims. Social media allows anyone to accuse a company of making false claims, and to attract a wide audience; this is one of many reasons to be scrupulously honest in all your claims.

Space on the Label

Understanding the value of these certifications, some companies have paid for multiple certifications covering different aspects. For instance, I'm looking at a 3-ounce (66-gram) bar of Theo 91%-cocoa chocolate that bears the following certifications and claims:

- ✓ USDA Organic, certified by Washington State Department of Agriculture

- ✓ Fair For Life social and fair-trade certified by IMO

- ✓ Charity partner (Audubon, benefiting Costa Rican cacao farmers and bird habitat)

- ✓ Kosher

- ✓ 50% recycled packaging

- ✓ Vegan

Of the four ingredients, all four are noted as organic, and all but vanilla are also marked fair trade.

That's a lot of information, not even counting a big panel of text about the charity project. Imagine trying to fit all that on a 1-ounce (22-gram) package label.

On one hand, you want to take full advantage of all the work you've done to get those multiple certifications you painstakingly earned—and on the other hand, you still want to create an attractive package with adequate white space and a great design, not cluttered up with a bunch of certification logos.

If that were my challenge, I might put text like this on the wrapper:

"Certified organic, fair trade, kosher and vegan. Benefits Audubon's forest, farm, and bird preservation efforts in Costa Rica. For more details, please scan this QR code into your smartphone, or visit www._____."

That way, you get all the good stuff out front, provide two ways for people who want all the details to get them—including the instant gratification made possible by the QR code—and still keep plenty of room on the label.

Why Greens **Hate** Hard-Sell

Imagine going down the road in your eco-friendly hybrid car (or better yet, your public transit conveyance or your bicycle), listening to some earnest musician's song about global warming. All of a sudden, this commercial is screaming at you:

Go green today! Act NOW to lock in your savings! Call 800-555-CASH or visit www.CashBackEnergySavings.com. That's 800-555-CASH or www.CashBackEnergySavings.com (note: phone and URL are fictional.

How do you feel about this loud, intrusive interruption?

Guess what—that's exactly how your prospects feel when they encounter hypey, in-your-face green marketing. And they tune it out. In fact, even well outside the green sector, obnoxious marketing is a lot less effective than it used to be. We have hundreds of thousands of sources for information now, and when one of them gets annoying, we leave.

Yes, there are companies out there doing this sort of thing—but no, it doesn't work very well.

Even more than the public as a whole, most segments of the green market are turned off by screamy hype. People who are drawn to green products and green lifestyles perceive themselves as thoughtful and intelligent, sorting out a range of competing (and sometimes conflicting) benefits and demerits to make choices that are good for the earth, and also good for themselves, their family, and their wallets.

And they are hungry for tools that help them make those decisions. They will demand that you provide the information they need in order to thoroughly evaluate for themselves whether your claims make sense and whether your offering is right for them. They will spend time reading articles, poring over back pages of websites, checking out your endorsements and testimonials, watching informational videos, scanning social media and blog feeds...and, especially, discussing planned major purchases with a cadre of trusted friends and associates.

To make it even more challenging, different sectors within that great big green market will bring different motivations and needs, and respond differently to the same marketing.

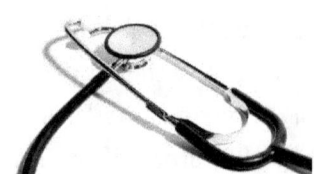

Let's look at one hypothetical typical green family. Children's health may be the primary concern of the mom, while her husband worries about the soaring cost of heating their home. His mother, who lives with them, has poor circulation and is cold all the time. The teenage daughter wants to make sure the workers involved are paid fair wages for harvesting the crops, but her younger brother is trying to find organic food that tastes good and doesn't seem weird to his classmates. If you try to reach all of these very different constituencies with the same marketing message, all of them will ignore you.

One way around that is to do different marketing pieces for each segment; Volkswagen and Apple are two companies that have always done that pretty well. Apple, for instance, markets one set of benefits to graphic artists, a different set to educators, and entirely different ones for musicians and film production people.

But for smaller companies, that approach may be expensive. A better alternative might be to *incorporate multiple marketing messages into the same communication.* Offer multiple pages on a website or brochure, multiple sections in a retail store, different series of informational documents aimed at different audiences.

For instance, a manufacturer of energy-efficient window quilts might create a website landing page offering the option to click to separate pages for high-end builders (looking for luxury features to differentiate their houses from others), interior designers (all about style), landlords (concerned with cost and appearance, and homeowners (balancing savings, durability, and their fashion statement). And those pages, in turn can subdivide by other interest areas.

Or, going back to our imaginary family, the company can market not only by professional affiliation but also by the particular interest. So a landing page might have links with titles like:

✓ How our window quilts can keep your family healthy and lower your medical bills (the mom will read that one)

- ✓ Why you're probably throwing away up to $800 every winter—through your windows (dad)

- ✓ The inside story of why we use only fair-trade cotton and how it's working miracles in the farming villages where we work (daughter)

- ✓ Looking to have the coolest room in town? Check out these awesome designs (son)

- ✓ How to stay nice and cozy-warm this winter without putting on a second and third sweater (that page is for grandma)

Next month, we'll look at the one of the best kinds of non-hype marketing: positioning yourself as the knowledgeable, helpful expert.

Build Your **Expert Reputation**, and Let Customers **Come to You**

Last month, we discussed why hypey, in-your-face marketing doesn't work for the green market, and looked at how to segment your marketing messages for different audiences. This month, let's take it a step further, and look at one of the most powerful (and least expensive) of all marketing methods: providing helpful, useful, actionable information that leads your prospect to consider you not only the expert, but the go-to company when they need what you do.

There are dozens of way to do this. You'll want to find the ones that are in tune with your audience's preferences and tastes. A few examples:

- ✓ Get in front of your best prospects as a speaker.

- ✓ Teach an ongoing course.

- ✓ Lead or be a featured guest on expert teleseminars, webinars, and chats.

- ✓ Join some Internet communities in your field of interest, and participate helpfully, answering questions and giving advice (this single strategy did more to turn my own business from a tiny consulting practice serving my own local area to the successful international business it is today).

✓ Prepare a series of White Papers or special reports illuminating certain confusing aspects of your industry and helping people make good decisions.

✓ Conduct a survey and release the results to major and trade media with some juicy summing-up quotes.

✓ Become a published author—publishing a book makes you an automatic expert, impresses a whole lot of people, and is much easier than it used to be.

✓ Get quoted in major media—not as hard as you may think—and then send the clips or links to your prospects.

✓ Create and distribute your own e-zine or printed newsletter (e-zine is greener and cheaper, but in some situations, print may be more effective)—and then later repurpose these articles by placing them on article banks such as ezinearticles.com or ideamarketers.com (if you have enough of these articles, and they categorize neatly, you can even turn them into a book later).

✓ Write your own blog and post to it at least twice a week (more is better).

✓ Be a guest blogger or columnist for other people's publications, including high-status expert sites like Examiner.com, Ask.com, and Triple Pundit.com.

✓ Share great articles, postcasts, studies, and other resources in your field on social media such as Twitter,

Google+, LinkedIn, and Facebook (two tips: First, no more than 10 to 20 percent of these resources should point to your own stuff—and second, software tools can automate some of this, for example automatically feeding your blog into your Facebook business page and LinkedIn profile).

Since the green market really craves information, as we discussed last month, you're actually doing your prospects a service by providing access to the information they seek. Provide the information, answers their questions, help them solve a problem or meet a need—and do it all with a friendly and approachable tone. And then it probably won't be long before your prospects start coming to you and saying things like, "I really enjoyed your article in Green Business Daily. Do you ever consult individually with retail stores? I'd like to hire you."

While old-fashioned push marketing is intrusive and even offensive, nobody gets offended when you simply place pertinent, helpful, well-written information in front of your prospects: information that's easy to access, easy to understand, and easy to implement.

What you're actually doing is creating a relationship and marketing based on that relationship. You build trust, confidence, and a sense that you can help with their problems or goals. And instead of going for the quick hit and expecting people to take action on the basis of interrupting them, you become a presence over time, showing up pleasurably in their mailboxes and social networks, and at the green conferences and trade shows they attend.

Another advantage is that unlike push marketers who have to pay to place their ads, you are reaching your prospects for free, and sometimes even getting paid to do your own marketing.

If you'd like help developing this type of marketing, don't be afraid to get in touch. I'm blessed that I actually enjoy strategizing on the best types of relationship marketing for you, and writing these kinds of materials.

The **WIIFM Factor** and
Green Marketing

When marketing green products and services to an eco-conscious audience, the most important question may be "How does this help the planet?"

But if you also want to reach people who are not committed greens, the most important question for them will be "What's in it for me?"

In the marketing world, "What's in it for me?" is often abbreviated as WIIFM. And since in the eastern half of the United States, radio station names are usually a group of four letters beginning with W—though some stations have three or five characters, some marketers joke that WIIFM is your prospect's "favorite radio station"—and you have to tune in if you want the sale.

Most of the time, you will want your marketing to reach both green and non-green markets—so that means you should be answering both questions, and answering them well. You want your marketing to convince these prospects that they and the planet will both be better off dealing with you and buying your offerings.

In other words, you want to combine planetary interest with self-interest.

That means, you might have to focus on such attributes as...

- ✓ The "cool" factor (a rooftop hydroponic garden, a sleek stainless steel reusable water bottle)

- ✓ Luxury or sportiness (how about the Tesla roadster, an electric car that looks like a Ferrari)

- ✓ Saving money (two-sided printers can save you about 40 percent of your paper costs)

- ✓ Comfort (better insulation or a much more efficient heating/air conditioning system means an end to cold and drafty winter nights, and some relief from sweltering summer days)

- ✓ Better health while getting close to nature (walking or running shoes, bicycles)

- ✓ Better health through avoiding toxics (natural cleaning and personal care products, organic clothing)

- ✓ Helping businesses and individuals comply with tighter laws and regulations, and to cover new areas such as Cradle-to-Cradle waste recovery; products and services that keep materials out of the waste stream, eliminate harmful chemicals, or reduce water and energy use will grow in popularit)

- ✓ Higher quality (buying local organic fruits and veggies and other gourmet foods from a farmers market, specialty store, or Community Supported Agriculture farm—once you've tasted the incredible burst of flavor from a locally grown, vine-ripened tomato, a hand-crafted cheese, or even a small-batch brewery beer, you may not ever want to buy the poor imitations at the supermarket)

How green is your customer? Outside of the super-green product arena where people really do make their purchase decisions to help the world (and are even willing to pay extra to get it), most people are going to fall somewhere in the middle of a continuum. Many people will buy a green offering if it's comparable in price, quality, and convenience, but won't pay much extra or incur extra hassle. If it's better than the conventional alternative, the sale is even easier.

Thus, if you can show that your t-shirts made from recycled soda bottles are at least as comfortable, durable, and affordable as a conventional non-organic cotton t-shirt, you should get the sale.

If you can show how your architect and your construction company can build a house so well insulated it doesn't need a furnace or air conditioner, using the savings to cover the cost of the energy improvements, you should get the sale

Combining self-interest with planetary interest means your marketing not only reaches both the green and non-green audiences, but it reaches them with both messages at the same time.

And thus, they will appeal strongly to people the audiences all along that continuum:

- ✓ Deep greens who feel guilty unless they can make an environmentally friendly choice

- ✓ People who are willing to go green, but not willing to inconvenience themselves (these are the folks in the middle)

✓ Those who don't care about green and may even be hostile, but recognize the superiority of your product

Once you've gone green while maintaining or increasing those qualities your buyers seek, your next job is to create marketing that tells that story, shows how your product or service is the most sensible and most exciting choice. (You'll find a lot of advice on that in my latest book, Guerrilla Marketing Goes Green.)

Going Global, Part 1:
Brand Identity in a Global
Economy

What's the first thing that comes into your head when someone says "Mercedes"?

If you're in Europe, I'll guess that you think of a company that has a car, truck, or bus for every market niche. In the United States— where General Motors, Ford, and Chrysler own that positioning— Mercedes brings up images of high-end sport and luxury cars; its competitors are companies like Porsche and Rolls-Royce, not Chevrolet or Dodge. (Ironically, Chrysler was actually owned by Mercedes' parent company, Daimler, from 1988-2007.) And in many other parts of the world, Mercedes is the workhorse of taxi, truck and bus fleets, supplying durable vehicles at affordable cost. In the Spanish-speaking world, Mercedes is also a popular female name, for which the car was named more than 100 years ago.

In short, the same brand has very different associations in different parts of the world. And this works in the green world, too: What's the first thing that comes into your head when someone says "Vitasoy"?

As a green business owner, you might be into natural foods—and you could know Vitasoy as a brand of organic soymilk, with various flavor options and a health consciousness. You might even know that the company owns several other soy-related brands, including Nasoya and Azumaya tofu products in the US and Unicurd in Singapore.

But in cultures like China, Hong Kong, and Latin America, their soymilks—under such names as Calci-Plus, Tsing Sum Zhan, and San Sui—are marketed as mainstream household beverages; packages I've seen in Latin American markets do not mention the word "organic."

Vitasoy's milk is called Soy Milky in Australia—a name that would not go over well in the United States.

In short, the same company has very different associations and very different product lines in different parts of the world.

Let's stay with green foods for another example: natural breakfast cereals. To a shopper in the United Kingdom, Weetabix® is a well-known and diverse line of cereals: the regular kind that's similar to shredded wheat...organic, crispy minis with chocolate, strawberries, peanut butter, or fruit and nuts...baked with golden syrup...chocolate (non-mini)...crunchy bran...and then variations made with different grains, such as Oatabix. There's even an o-shaped imitation of Cheerios. But in the US, it's unusual to see anything other than the basic biscuits, sold as a green product.

What's the point? It's that large companies—in the green world or in the general consumer marketplace—go after different markets, and market differently, in different parts of the world, or in different market segments within the same country.

In fact, smart companies segment much more closely than by country. Within 16 kilometers (10 miles) of my house, the same supermarket chain has stores in four communities. Walking the aisles, you'd think they were different companies entirely. Two are geared toward the adventurous tastes of healthy-living folks in the nearby college towns, with a lot of natural products, green packaging, exotic local fruits and vegetables, and so on. And one of those, in a more international community, has an Asian foods section that's bigger than some Asian grocery stores. The third, in a heavily Hispanic city, has a product selection geared to Puerto Rican tastes.

 And the fourth, in a working-class city that hosts a large military base, is the land of packaged, bland convenience foods for a burger-and-pasta-salad crowd. It would be hard to find anything organic on that store's shelves.

You'll find examples of this kind of segmentation in industry after industry. Even something like book cover design will be startlingly different for the same book in different parts of the world.

If you read this column, you're probably not a giant multinational company with resources to create different product variations all over the world.

But these days, all of us are global businesses. As a green marketing consultant and copywriter working solo from a farmhouse in the northeastern United States, I've not only served clients from all parts of my own country, but also all across Asia and Europe: Japan, Cyprus, Israel, England, France, Germany, Belgium, and elsewhere. And this column runs in Australia and Asia, as well as in the United States.

If an international client comes to me to reach the green market in the United States, that's easy for me. But if that client wants to reach an audience in a different market, I have to find ways to put myself in the mindset of a potential customer who thinks very differently from me, and that can be a challenge.

For me, the way around this is to focus on the slices of the market that play to my core strengths. For instance, if a company wants to reach the green consumer, or market green products and services to either green or nongreen audiences, my subject knowledge is strong enough to make up for the cultural differences.

If you want to go into different markets, ask yourself questions like these:

- ✓ What do you offer that a customer can't find at home already?

- ✓ How will you deal with shipping, customs, and tariff costs, and will you be able to compete after factoring those in?

- ✓ Who will sell and service your products in that country?

- ✓ How might a tweak in the product, packaging, or marketing make it more attractive in that market?

✓ How does entering this far-away market make the world better or address environmental and social problems— and how can you use that commitment in your marketing?

Good luck! And if you need guidance on this journey, feel free to contact me.

Going Global, Part 2: Creating **Positioning** for **Global Brands**

Last month, we looked at when it might make sense to enter a global market with your green product or service. This month, we'll take a look at market positioning that might make it worth the hassle and expense of entering new countries.

Your Unique Selling Proposition, or USP, is marketing-speak for the factor that makes your offering special enough to win over buyers who either have been meeting the need elsewhere or didn't realize they needed your product or service. If you're entering a different country, your USP will have to be clear and convincing enough that people will switch.

In the world of green products and services, you'll construct your USP based in either or both of two different themes: how the product or service improves your customer's life (solves a problem, meets a need, fulfills a desire)—and how it helps others and the world. While customers who already think green are receptive to the second, to reach people other than committed greens, you also need positioning points in the first category.

A few possibilities:

Higher Standards

I've been amazed for several years that European cosmetics and personal care product companies haven't stormed the US with an appeal to consumer safety, i.e., "Because we're based in Spain, we have to meet European Union standards for product safety. These standards are much tougher than those in the United States, and that's your guarantee that our shampoos are safe and healthy for your children." This is a market opportunity waiting to be captured, and the early movers could have quite a leg up, particularly following the scares about safety issues in imported Chinese goods. Yet even European companies like The Body Shop that do have a presence in the US fail to capitalize on this in their marketing.

Standards in health, the environment (organic, biodegradable packaging, waste recapture, no animal testing, etc.), ease of use, etc. all make great positioning points.

Economic Opportunity for the Poor

If, say, your product is sourced from organic biodynamic fair-trade ingredients, that gives you bragging rights. While many consumers around the world recognize that fair trade, organic, and biodynamic are good things, they may not recognize exactly what it means. You, as the product manufacturer, importer, or marketer, must educate them. Your customers and prospects need to know that buying from you means not only a living wage to the farmer, but also:

Certification that child slaves are not used (an especially big issue in the cocoa industry)

A pool of money to the village cooperative, which uses it for democratically decided improvement projects such as building wells—and that in turn means teenage girls are able to stay in school because they're not spending half the day carrying pitchers of water several miles

Money that stays in the local producer communities and is not 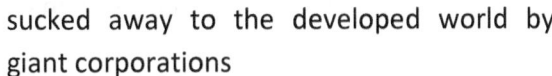 sucked away to the developed world by giant corporations

 Sustainable farming practices that mean the harvest will continue for many years, because the soil is nurtured, not depleted, and the farms use companion planting rather than destructive monocropping

The consumer is spared exposure to harmful chemicals, and gets to savor a food product that still contains its original nutrients and thus offers both higher nutritional content and better flavor

When you present things this way, you provide good reasons to buy from you instead of some commoditized agribusiness firm. Wouldn't any smart consumer want to make a choice like that?

And there are other types of appeals on social-betterment grounds. Companies like Khaya Cookies in South Africa <www.khayacookies.com/> or Greyston Bakery in the United States <www.greystonbakery.com/> make a big point of providing jobs to people who would otherwise be unemployable: young mothers in the townships outside Johannesburg, and ex-offenders or people with mental disabilities from the slums of New York, respectively.

Deeper Environmental Benefits

What do your green attributes *really* mean? Less intensive use of water, energy or materials and reduced or recaptured waste output can mean lower prices to the consumer, reduced contribution to catastrophic climate change, more productive farmland, etc. Are these important enough to get consumers to switch from a home-country brand to your export? And will the  differences make up for the environmental impact of shipping something halfway across the world?

The Key Concept: Make Your Story Meaningful

When you bring a product to market in a different country, the marketing challenge is to tell "the story behind the story"—to make it come alive with your commitment to a better world that is so strong it has brought you all the way across an ocean to do business. This kind of marketing is a good thing even in the domestic market, but with the extra challenges of going global, it's crucial. Keep asking, "what does this mean? Why is it important? Why should my customer care?"

And once again, you don't have to go it alone. People like me are happy to help you succeed.

Publicity, Part 1: Should You Seek Mainstream **Media Publicity** for Your Green Business?

 Publicity uses traditional and new media—such as newspapers, magazines, newsletters, blogs, radio, podcasts, and television—to get the word out about your product, service, and/or ideas—not by paying for advertising, but by becoming part of the content.

There are many ways to get media publicity. Examples include (among many others) an article about your product or service, or that at least mentions you, in either the news or feature pages...a profile of your business...an announcement of an event you're doing...an interview with you on TV or radio...a reporter covering your product launch press conference. It brings visibility, credibility, opportunity, and sales.

Publicity provides the seal of approval of a trusted outside source: a journalist. Like testimonials and awards, this third-party validation helps you stand out in a crowded marketplace. And of course, it also means that a lot more people hear about you. Not only will people see the newscast, read the publication, or hear you on the radio, but in many cases you can quote from the publicity in your own marketing materials, link to it on your website, and generally maximize the impact to your benefit.

Put yourself in your prospect's shoes for a moment: if you're trying to choose a vendor, and you visit one website that shows the product has been covered in the Sydney Morning Herald in Australia, the Business Times in Kuala Lumpur, Malaysia, and the Boston Globe in the United States—but the other websites you visit don't mention any press—which are you more likely to choose?

The Tradeoff: Credibility vs. Control

When you get free publicity rather than pay for advertising, you give up control over the content. The news media can write what they want, and you may have to deal with correcting inaccuracies later. But you have the added legitimacy of being chosen to represent your field.

And because news coverage at least pretends to be unbiased, it is more valuable than advertising; you get, in a sense, a testimonial—a disinterested, credible party who thinks you're worthy of positive attention. Many people take news coverage more seriously than advertising—and may be more likely to be influenced by it than by a paid ad. This is particularly true these days, as ads not only have less credibility than they used to, but are often bypassed entirely, as new technologies allow them to be skipped.

For green businesses, publicity has many additional advantages:

✓ Publicity helps you introduce complex concepts to new audiences. If, for instance, you run a zero-waste factory, or build homes that don't need a furnace or air conditioning system, a good article can make it clear that these "impossible" achievements are actually quite possible.

✓ News coverage educates the public about environmental issues. From climate change to recycling, the press helps citizens understand the wider issues, and how they play out locally.

✓ When you tell your story in the news media, you can differentiate your business from not-so-green competitors.

✓ And sometimes, publicity leads to more contacts that advance your career: a company president sees the article and decides you're the perfect consultant to transition that company to renewable energy and green manufacturing...a meeting planner contacts you to see whether you could speak at a conference in front of 200 of your best prospects...a different journalist sees the story and wants to cover you as well. In short, the media coverage can become a doorway to far more lucrative ventures.

Oh yes, and don't forget that every now and then, an article or a TV or radio interview can actually motivate people to go out and buy your product then and there! Especially if you make it easy by including your website, your phone number and some kind of special offer.

Publicity, Part 2: What Kinds of Messages Can Bring You **Mainstream Media Publicity**?

We touched very lightly last month on the types of activity that can bring you coverage in traditional media. This month, we'll go into more detail, and then next month, I'll share resources that help you get coverage.

First of all, if what you know about news-worthy activities is more than five years old, the very first thing you need to do is update your knowledge. In the not-so-distant past, activities like publishing a book or CD, launching a new website, introducing a new  product, or speaking at a minor conference were often enough to get coverage—but not anymore.

In today's world of short attention spans, information bombardment, and a news system that focuses on drama and celebrity much more than on life-changing developments in science and technology or even on the real issues that modern nations face, those types of accomplishments are not enough anymore. For example, tens of millions of books are published every year—and that means it's a lot harder to get publicity for a new book than it was 20 years ago, when the worldwide total was probably under a million (42,217 books were published just in the United States in 1993, compared with more than 3 million in 2010). So if you've written a book about zero-waste manufacturing, it won't be enough anymore to send your local newspaper a press release with the headline, "Green Manufacturing Expert Publishes New Book." Reporters keep their fingers right near the delete key as they scan hundreds of press releases arriving in their inboxes, and that one won't make the cut.

In today's world, you have to be much more effective in telling your green story: *you have to think like a journalist!* And an overwhelmed journalist with a supercrowded inbox and four stories to research and write on a typical work day, at that.

Journalists are looking at what sells newspapers, cable TV accounts, and radio ads. They look at their readers' pain points, problems, aspirations, and goals—even better if there's a tie-in with hot news stories or celebrities.

So you must market your green products and services the same way. Focus on the problems you solve, the benefits your customers achieve, or the entertainment value you create—along with your credibility. Thus, a better headline would be something like "Manufacturers Can Slash Disposal Costs by 80 Percent While Opening New Markets, Bestselling Author Claims." That's a headline that will make a business journalist want to read more.

Similarly, if your CEO makes a speech at a conference, focus on the message within the speech; if a reporter sees a headline like "ExxonMobil CEO: Climate Change is the Most Crucial Issue of Our

Time," it's going to get a lot more attention than "Oil Company Executive Addresses Conference of Drill Bit Dealers." (That example is completely hypothetical—but I would love to read in the press about a major oil company's commitment to addressing climate change—particularly ExxonMobil, which has funded many studies that question climate change.)

So here are some results-focused "pegs" that you can use to convert your publicity outreach into news coverage, even for the sorts of events that are no longer news by themselves:

- ✓ Solving one or more problems

- ✓ Producing benefits not just to customers but to other stakeholders (for instance, the benefit of Fair Trade food products is the economic boost to the producer community, which in turn becomes more able to buy other goods and services)

- ✓ Achieving and quantifying a major green milestone such as 60 percent reduced emissions or 100-percent-recycled raw materials

- ✓ Setting a major environmental goal or policy statement, especially one that the mainstream business world would consider difficult or impossible

- ✓ Creating a whole new product category (very common in the green market: an enzyme that means you don't have to flush as often, a vertical garden space for apartment dwellers, a wheelchair transporter no bigger than a Smart or a Fiat 500, to name three actual products)

And if you have trouble thinking up creative, benefit-driven news pegs, don't be afraid to call in an expert. Lots of people, including me, can write a terrific press release for you.

Publicity, Part 3:
How to Get Publicity

Imagine for a moment that you get your hometown newspaper, open up the business page, and are happily stunned to see a big article about you and your work.

Now imagine that it's not your hometown newspaper—it's actually 5000 miles/8000 kilometers away from where you live.

Thrilled? You should be! I certainly was when I saw this photo, featuring my book cover in an article about my ideas and the talk I was doing the following week.

I've been similarly thrilled to see "my name in lights" in such places as the New York Times, the Wall Street Journal, Entrepreneur Magazine, and even Woman's Day, each of which have cited me multiple times. And even more thrilled to see coverage around the world...in major publications in Australia, Romania, Colombia, and elsewhere. I even had my book cover blasted across an electronic billboard in New York's Times Square. And I'm especially thrilled since none of this media attention cost me even one penny.

It also gladdens my heart that when I get this kind of coverage, it means more people are learning that green and ethical business can be profitable business—that all of us, together, are creating a new, earth-centered business paradigm. And it doesn't hurt that my high media visibility sometimes brings in a new client or speaking invitation.

In a typical year, I do 50 to 150 interviews in print, Internet, and broadcast media. I do this without a public relations agency, and without a corporate presence; I am simply one solopreneur working from a farmhouse in a rural area.

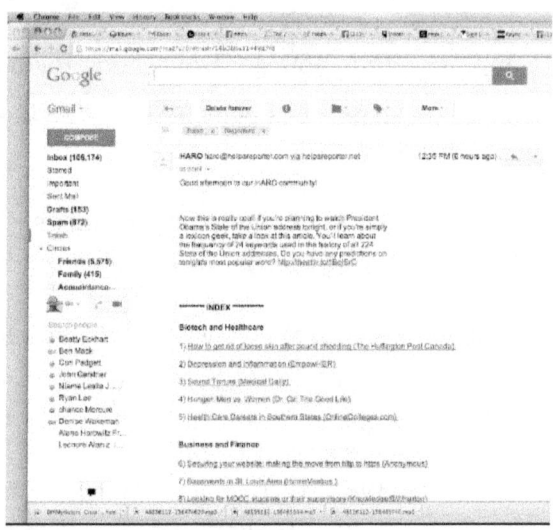

HARO (Help A Reporter Out) www.helpareporter.com
(the above screenshot shows part of a HARO table of contents)

Would you like to get free exposure for your business? It's not that hard.

We talked about press releases earlier in this series. The Kauai writeup came from a press release sent by the meeting organizer who brought me in.

But there's an even better way to get in front of reporters: *offer to be a source for reporters who are already looking for story sources for a specific article.* Conveniently, there are several no-cost services that match reporters looking for sources with sources seeking coverage:

- ✓ HARO (Help A Reporter Out): www.helpareporter.com

- ✓ Reporter Connection: www.ReporterConnection.com

- ✓ Pitch Rate: www.PitchRate.com

- ✓ Radio Guest List: www.RadioGuestList.com

Sign up for some or all of these, follow the Twitter feeds of @helpareporter, @reporterconxn, @pitchrate, @profnet, @prleads, and @radioguestlist—and pitch when you match the criteria the reporter requests (DON'T spam them with inappropriate responses, unless you want to get banned).

Now, some pitching hints to turn queries into coverage:

- ✓ Respond as instantly as possible (except for Radio GuestList—in most cases, the radio producers have an ongoing need, and you'll stand out more by waiting a week or two until the deluge dies down). These queries may draw 200 responses, so the fastest in get the closest consideration. Consider setting up a separate e-mail address to receive and respond to queries, and check that account every hour from 6 a.m. to 6 pm. US Eastern Time (or better yet, turn on audio notification just for that account).

- ✓ Stay on topic and relevant—don't try to make a fit where one doesn't really exist. That means paying attention to such factors as geographic needs, size of company, or anything else the reporter might specify in the query (yeah, it would be nice if more reporters put the restrictions in the headline).

- ✓ Give the reporter something to quote right in your query (I usually do between 2-5 bullet points or one very meaty paragraph).

- ✓ Mention your relevant credentials and include a link to your media room on your website.

- ✓ Set up Google and Yahoo Alerts for your name, book title, and perhaps main topic keywords (if not too general), so you can see if you get quoted—reporters won't always tell you.

What goes in a media room? Anything a reporter might find useful in researching a story, such as photos for reprint, a list of media that have covered you, press releases, a bio, and—very important for radio or TV—sample interview questions. You can see one of my media rooms at http://greenandprofitable.com/contact/media-room/#media —you're welcome to use it as a model.

Publicity, Part 4:
But Social Media is Different:
10 **Social Media Marketing**
Success Principles

Just as marketing through free publicity is different than marketing via paid advertising or your own channels, marketing on social media—sites like Twitter, Facebook, LinkedIn, and Pinterest—is different as well. I could easily put together a list of 100 tips, but let's keep it simple and just do ten.

1. See the Big Picture

Social media provides a powerful toolkit to change the discourse—so instead of wasting space on what you ate for breakfast, post content designed to influence other people (Facebook-style visual memes, even if they're nothing but quotes, are great for this). At the same time, remember to be human. Show some parts of your personality, mention your own life events, and offer congrats or condolences when you have the chance.

2. Skip the Hard-Sell

Avoid skewing toward blatant "buy my stuff" self-promotion—unless you want 90% of your followers to leave and the remaining 10% to be spambots. I recommend no more than 1 totally self-promotional post every 20 posts.

3. Your Posts Live Forever

Social media is a *permanent* record. Never post anything that will embarrass you later; drunken-idiot pictures may be fun at the party, but don't look so good when college turns into job-application time. Even if you go back and delete a post, it could come back to haunt you, because the content will still be accessible to people who know how to hunt for it.

4. Small is Beautiful

Even Twitter's 140 characters is plenty if you combine a compelling headline with a link to the full article and/or post a picture.

5. The Social Media Success Formula

You need two things to succeed in social media: content...and audience! Content is the easy part. If you want people to follow you, go out and build an audience, *organically*. You do this by following people of influence, interacting with them, sharing their posts, commenting (appropriately—this is NOT an invitation to spam) not just on their social media but on their blogs, commenting on the comments made about your own posts, sharing your lists of people to follow, etc.

6. Understand Social Media's Strengths and Limitations

The power of social media is the way messages can spread to friends of friends of friends—people you couldn't have reached directly. Some of them will start following you; some you can engage in dialog with. But the flaw of social media is the way you often don't see the same people consistently, and who you do see is very arbitrary depending on when you happen to sign on. Tools like HootSuite or TweetDeck provide partial fixes; for instance, they allow you to set up a column that tracks people you want to follow more closely. Also use a social media tool to schedule your posts for maximum impact, autopost to social media every time you put up a new blog post, and post to more than one network with a couple of clicks.

7. The "Secret Sauce" of Mainstream Social Media

Participation in subcommunities such as LinkedIn groups and Facebook pages is another way to overcome this limitation. Pick two or three that reach at least 500 of your best prospects, have high discussion quality, and a good number of people actively participating

8. The Even Bigger Secret—Back from the 1990s

Similarly, find some old-style email-based discussion lists (for example, on yahoogroups.com); these are much less popular than they used to be, but they put you in front of the same audience of prime prospects over and over again, and usually allow you to include at least a short email signature that includes a slogan, link to your website, and your contact information.

9. Bring Them Back to You

Let social media work in tandem with media you control; do not let social media platforms exclusively own your best content; draw people to something where the rug can't be pulled out from under you, such as a blog on your own domain.

10. Keep the Content Alive

Remember that only a tiny fraction of your followers/friends will see any particular post. So don't be afraid to post the content again—but word it differently, and have several other posts in between, so you don't look like an a-hole if someone goes to your profile page. On Facebook, you can also keep your important posts in other people's streams longer (with this week's algorithms, anyway) by going back and commenting on them—so have a dialog with the people who comment on your post, but maybe an hour or so later.

Convince on Climate Change with Nonenvironmental Arguments

Recently, the UK newspaper The Guardian argued that activists could get more traction with nongreens on climate change by pointing out the public health consequences of failing to act.[1]

And that's certainly true—but it's nowhere near the whole story.

Over a year ago, in my April, 2012 column, I wrote about marketing green products to nongreen audiences. I talked about finding the what's-in-it-for-me factor so that nongreens want to buy green products because they're  more hip, or cheaper, or more luxurious, etc. And I've been pointing this out in my Making Green Sexy talks for at least three years.

Now we have to take that same way of thinking and shift it from the material world—products and services—to the less tangible realm of what kind of world they want to live in, what kind of world they want to leave to their children and grandchildren.

---

1   http://www.guardian.co.uk/sustainable-business/climate-change-environment-health-problem

Because these folks don't generally consider human impact on the earth, save-the-planet arguments won't carry much water with them.

But we can gain converts to the clause of reversing catastrophic climate change on several grounds that are not blatant appeals to environmentalism, among them:

- ✓ Economics

- ✓ Health (as The Guardian pointed out)

- ✓ Lifestyle

- ✓ Let's look at each of these in turn.

Economics

The longer we wait to reverse catastrophic climate change, the more expensive it will be. I could fill this entire column with numerous economic arguments for addressing climate change NOW, and still only scratch the surface. Here are a few positive-focused and negative-focused arguments:

- ✓ Avoiding the enormous costs of cleaning up after climate-change-related storms like Hurricanes Katrina, Rita, Irene, and Sandy (many trillions of dollars)—and after messy oil spills like Exxon Valdez and BP Deepwater Horizon

- ✓ Switching to clean, renewable energy sources stops the transfer of wealth from individual consumers to oil barons and big banks, and from industrialized nations to countries that can be hostile to the modern world

- ✓ Saying goodbye to paying energy bills, because you can harness free energy from the sun, wind, tides, etc.

- ✓ Keeping global temperatures where they belong means lower costs for air conditioning and heating.

- ✓ Paying lower taxes if we no longer need the military to secure fossil fuel sources

Health

- ✓ Getting off coal will reduce asthma, emphysema, and other breathing diseases.

- ✓ Too much heat is a public health issue. Remember the summer of 2003, when thousands of people died in Europe's heat wave?

- ✓ Natural gas fracking and tar sands oil extraction put our water supply at severe risk. Water pollution ruins not just our drinking water but also water for agriculture, medicine, food packaging, etc.

Lifestyle

- ✓ Transporting ourselves by bicycle or on our own two feet offers the benefits of cardiovascular exercise: appropriate weight, fitness, increased endurance, longevity, etc. If that's not practical, using mass transit at least converts stressy driving time to time you can do something non-stressful and enjoyable, like read a book or watch a movie.

- ✓ Crops or animals that depend on cold weather, like maple syrup or polar bears, are at risk if it doesn't get cold enough. At the same time, pests like mosquitoes and ticks will provide year-round misery without a frost to kill them off for the winter.

- ✓ We all feel happier when we base more of our diet on local, sustainable foods. It's not just that they have less of a carbon footprint because they don't have to be transported great distances. The arguments that will persuade nongreens are how much better they taste, how many more nutrients are accessible in really fresh foods, and—among the more forward-thinking—how much more of a boost buying local provides to the local economy.

There are probably several other categories of talking points where greens can reach out to nongreens. In all of it, we need to focus on the direct benefits to the people we're talking about, who may not be committed greens. To put it another way, we need to reach each person with the arguments that resonate with that specific person.

Let's all go out and convince a few people!

[1]. *http://www.guardian.co.uk/sustainable-business/climate-change-environment-health-problem*

If You've **Gone Green**—
Remember to **Brag**

Looking out over the fields of the farm I live on, I always smile when I see our luscious organic garden. Once, when we had a particularly bountiful harvest of hot peppers, I went to the garden, picked five pounds of surplus, and brought the whole big bag to my neighbors' farmstand. They sell produce from a bunch of local farms, usually labeled with the farm of origin and the town, and of course, the price.

So I was figuring mine would go out with something like "Grown right here on this farm by our neighbors, with no pesticides or chemical fertilizers" and the price per pound. (They couldn't legally call our homegrown veggies organic, because for our home garden, we don't go through any certification process.) With a sign like that, I would have expected my chiles to go flying out the door, and I would have had a steady market for the remaining two months of the season.

That was the theory. But for some reason, instead of displaying them proudly at the front of the store with the rest of the local vegetables, instead of trumpeting their purity and hyperlocalism, they put my beautiful peppers in an out-of-the-way spot, with no sign at all. And there, they slowly shriveled over the next week or so. Needless to say, I didn't bring them any more to sell.

Here are the two marketing lessons the farmstand forgot:

- ✓ When your product or service has attributes that are demonstrably superior, announce those attributes to the world. As it happens, our area has a very strong awareness about the importance of buying local foods and the superiority of fresh/local/organic. And the farmstand, located in a rural area close to three college towns, caters to this educated market with a wide range of local and fair trade products. Failing to label my peppers was an act of self-sabotage, because this aware demographic had no idea what made the peppers special, and therefore they didn't choose to purchase them. After all, if your sets of benefits don't convince you that you have a better offering, why will they convince anyone else?

- ✓ Make it easy for your customers to get the information they need. Failing to put a price on the display meant that anyone considering the peppers would have to go to the counter and ask—and that extra step is a disincentive.

A less personal example: I know of a household paper products company that began making its paper products from recycled raw materials all the way back in 1950. When Earth Day first happened back in 1970 and society began to be much more conscious of environmental issues, this company was perfectly placed to capitalize on the rapidly growing trend by pointing out that they had switched to recycled paper 20 years earlier.

Unfortunately, that thought apparently did not occur to them, and certainly they didn't put it into action. It was about 30 more years after the first Earth Day—and 50 years after the switch—before the company started even mentioned recycled on its labels, and all the way to 2009 before the company really turned this into a marketing asset.

Not surprisingly, once the company finally started actively bragging, it rapidly became the #1 selling recycled brand in the country, even though its only available in one region of the country.

I have learned not to be shy about listing the benefits of my own offerings. So let me remind you: If you'd like to know more about smart green marketing, pick up a copy of my award-winning and Environmental category bestselling eighth book, Guerrilla Marketing Goes Green: Winning Strategies to Improve Your Profits and Your Planet (co-authored with Jay Conrad Levinson). In addition to getting great advice about how to market green products and services, and how to move toward a greener future, you'll also receive $2000 worth of bonuses if you register your purchase (no matter where you buy it) at <www.guerrillamarketinggoesgreen.com/resources-2/bonuses>.

What **Green Marketers**
Can Learn from **Ring Tones**

 Every mobile phone comes with some ringtones built in. And therefore, nobody actually needs to purchase a ringtone. And yet, at its peak, continuing at least through 2011, the ringtone industry generated more than $4 billion a year (US dollars), worldwide. (The industry is declining, as text supplants voice, and as more phones carry greater options in standard ringer choices.)

$4 billion is a lot of money for something that nobody needs.

Are there lessons in this industry for green marketers? Most certainly. Here are a two among many:

1. We Crave Making Our Mark

The age of individuality goes back at least as far as the Beatnik movement in the 1950s, flowered with the hippies of the 1960s, and continues to spread in our own era. As a society, we each strive to be seen as unique, different.

The conformity of the 1950s gray flannel suit is long gone. Where once there were rules of fashion, now, we have enormous latitude in what we wear. We can mix colors and patterns that would make our parents cringe. Women might wear a miniskirt over a mid-length dress, with leggings underneath. Men have added pink and lavender to their shirt choices.

And perhaps even more than in society as a whole, the green world is populated by people who declare their individuality—not just the off-grid recluse with a two-foot-long beard and a shack made from old car parts, but the suburban housewife who wears upcycled fashion jewelry made from old blue jeans and discarded CDs...the craft brewery customer who seeks out an artisan beer that uses fresh organic grain supplied by a local farmer...the college student who proudly bicycles to class...

We business owners benefit when we celebrate our customers' individuality.

Toyota had to learn that lesson the hard way. When the Prius was first introduced as a drab sedan with limited color choices, sales were slow. From the car's introduction in 1997 through the end of the original model six years later, only about 123,000 were sold.

When the now-familiar sleek hatchback with its wide variety of color choices was brought to market in 2004, sales jumped dramatically, to 1,192,000 in its 4-year lifespan. In other words, it sold nearly ten times as many, in 2/3 the time. All of a sudden, the car was considered sexy.

The trend continued into the 3rd generation, still in production and including various newer models, including the plug-in, small wagon, and midsize wagon. After four years, Toyota has sold more than 2.3 of them.

2. We will Pay for Practical Value

There is a very practical reason why some people choose to buy a ringtone: they get tired of hearing a ring just like theirs, reaching madly for the phone, and discovering that it was someone else's.

To put this in a green context, I sampled some natural tooth-rinse at a green festival, and liked it enough to buy a container at the show. I've been pleased with the way it makes my mouth feel after daily use, and when I ran out, I bought more. I paid $13.99 for a bottle of fluid that's basically food-grade hydrogen peroxide with peppermint oil. I could probably make my own for two or three dollars, if I could easily locate a source of food-grade peroxide. Or I could go the drug store and buy ordinary peroxide for even less. But it is worth it to me to know that they've tested the formula and got it right, to know they've gone through safety procedures and have packaged it in a way that's convenient to use.

So if you give people reasons based on convenience and practicality, they will buy from you, just as they've bought ringtones.

The **Opinions** of **Others**

On a recent trip to New York, we decided to have dinner at our favorite Tibetan restaurant. But we only got as far as the front door.

New York, for several years now, not only grades the sanitation of its tens of thousands of eateries with an A, B, or C, but requires them to post the grade in plain view of the entrance. And this place, where we'd enjoyed several wonderful meals, had been downgraded to a C.

This in a Queens neighborhood that boasts over 100 interesting ethnic restaurants within easy walking distance.

So instead of eating Tibetan, we chose an Indian vegetarian restaurant that we'd also eaten at previously.

The loss of our business is a lesson in third-party validation. If you're in an industry that offers third-party ranking or certification, people will pay attention to how well you rank or whether you do or don't have the certification.

In the green world, numerous sectors offer certifications that matter. Food businesses can be certified organic, GMO-free, fairly traded, etc.

Buildings and building products can be LEED certified at several different levels.

Green businesses of any type in the US can get certified by Green America, whose silver level is easy to achieve, but whose gold level takes quite a bit of work. (I'm proud to say that my own marketing consulting and copywriting firm was the first business ever to achieve Green America's gold certification, so I speak from direct personal experience.)

 Independent certification is a particularly strong reason to do business together—because a good certification shows that you met independent standards put forth by a theoretically neutral and third party. Note, however, that self-certification will only convince those who can't see through the scheme. You want it come from an outside party.

Certification is a powerful offer of social proof. Social proof is showing that others have made this choice, thus implying that it's a good choice to make. This is why businesses sometimes park employees' vehicles in the customer lot, or run ads with headlines like "98,762 homeowners can't be wrong." (Actually, they could be quite wrong. But that's a discussion for another column.)

In our unvetted society, where the barriers to entry in starting a company, publishing a book, recording a music album, or inventing a new green process have gotten so low that pretty much anyone can do these things, social proof becomes a set of important judging criteria that allow your prospects to sift the offers and choose the ones that are likely to offer quality.

But certification is only one type of social proof among many. You probably already know dozens of ways to get social proof. Here are a few:

- ✓ Reviews in mainstream media

- ✓ Reader reviews on consumer sites

- ✓ Awards

- ✓ Endorsements or testimonials, especially from people who are famous (the most believable identify the actual person's name—not just initials—city, and title/company)

- ✓ Speaking before prestigious organizations

- ✓ Landing a publishing or recording contract with one of the legacy book publishers or recording companies

- ✓ Being interviewed or publishing your own articles in the media

- ✓ Large numbers of engaged followers on social media such as Twitter, LinkedIn, Facebook, and Pinterest

- ✓ Having a Wikipedia page

Actually, my own Wikipedia page is a great example of the power of social proof. Of course, I wanted the page up there to create social proof. But one of the thousands of citizen-editors challenged my page and said it should be taken down because it was too promotional. What got him to back down was when another editor cited the social proof that I've been quoted repeatedly in the New York Times (widely considered the most authoritative newspaper in the United States and among the top newspapers in the world).

I enjoyed writing this column from 2010 to 2014, and I think I provided very high value for those who read it. Unfortunately, I never got enough markets to make the project economically viable.

As I move in the direction of helping companies see the value in solving problems like hunger, poverty, war, and climate catastrophe, I can no longer afford the luxury of doing this column for the few markets that subscribed. So this will be the last issue for a while.

I'd love to bring it back, if I can get to a minimum number of subscribers each paying just $10 per month. If you have possible markets for me, please drop me a line at shel AT greenandprofitable.com with the subject "Column Market."

Disclaimer: The very observant among you may notice that some examples come up more than once. Keep in mind that this ebook is a compilation of a monthly column that ran for four years. I have organized the columns by topic rather than chronologically here, and as a result, columns that may have been years apart end up close to each other in the same ebook. Yes, some examples are repeated, but they were inserted to make different points, at different times. Please also note that nothing in this ebook series should be taken as legal or professional advice, and as in any situation, your results may vary as you implement the tips and ideas.

About Shel Horowitz and
Business For a Better World

Green business profitability expert Shel Horowitz shows businesses how to profit both by going green and by addressing problems like hunger and poverty, war, violence, and catastrophic climate change. Active in both marketing and the environment since his teen years in the early 1970s, Shel is the award-winning author of eight books including long-running Amazon category bestseller _Guerrilla Marketing Goes Green_.

- ✓ As a consultant, Shel brings laser focus to turning problems into opportunities, opening new markets, and helping you identify potential partners.

- ✓ As a marketing and informational copywriter trained in journalism, Shel is known for his clear writing, ability to make technical concepts accessible, and his skill in telling "the story behind the story" to move people to action.

- ✓ As an international speaker and trainer, Shel combines dynamic vocal style with powerful graphics and gets his audiences actively involved. He's spoken at major business and environmental conferences in locations as diverse as Istanbul, Davos (Switzerland), and Honolulu.

After over a decade actively assisting green businesses with their marketing, Shel branched out in 2014 to help businesses seize profit opportunities in turning hunger and poverty into sufficiency, war and violence into peace, and catastrophic climate change into planetary balance—and helping individuals reclaim their power to actively create this better world.

Shel is happy to talk to you about helping in any of these areas. Reach him at 413-586-2388 (8 a.m. to 10 p.m. US Eastern Time), email shel AT greenandprofitable.com,or find him on Twitter @ShelHorowitz.

Shel also has a gift for you: a free copy of his ebook, *Painless Green: 111 Tips to Help the Environment, Lower Your Carbon Footprint, Cut Your Budget, and Improve Your Quality of Life—With No Negative Impact on Your Lifestyle*. To claim your free copy of this $9.95 ebook, visit PainlessGreenBook.com/earthday and use the code, G&Pebook.

One more set of gifts, FREE with your no-cost subscription to Shel Horowitz's monthly Clean and Green Newsletter:

- ✓ Seven Tips to Gain Marketing Traction as a Green Guerrilla

- ✓ Seven Weeks to a Greener Business: once a week for seven weeks, tips on going greener with printing, energy saving, waste reduction, water conservation, transportation, going deep-green, and of course, green marketing.

- ✓ Plus the informative monthly newsletter, published since 1997 and featuring a business tip or profile plus a book review each issue.

Sign up in the upper-right-hand corner at http://greenandprofitable.com.

Green and Profitable

BOOK 3

Policy and Ethics Issues
For Green Businesses

Shel Horowitz

How Do You **Balance** Conflicting Environmental **Priorities**?

What do you do when there's no clear eco-friendly choice—when you have to balance competing claims of environmental benefit against competing harms?

In January [2011], I spoke at the Sustainable Foods Summit in San Francisco. My challenge to the other attenders was to achieve a food system that combines the artisan quality and chemical/petroleum independence of pre-20th century food production with the massive volume and ability to feed hungry people of the 20th century Green Revolution, while achieving the distribution necessary to end hunger.

Conflicting Priorities

That sounds great, in theory. But how do we get there? And what trade-offs do we have to make along the way?

Some of the other speakers had their own ideas about the rocky road ahead, not just in food sustainability but a host of related issues. Among the many concerns they raised:

✓ Is it better to switch to no-till farming, which dramatically alleviates soil erosion but is very difficult to do without herbicides—or to build up soil quality naturally through organic or biodynamic methods, and hope that the soil doesn't blow away in the meantime?

✓ What is the real benefit of using biodegradable plastics (such as compostable cutlery or packaging) if the sources of corn or potatoes for these plastics are genetically modified plants? And when food is scarce in many parts of the world, do we really want to divert cropland from food to plastic (or energy) production?

✓ Which is more sustainable: a lightweight plastic bag made from virgin materials (i.e., petroleum), or a plastic clamshell using 40 times as much material, but made from recycled water bottles?

Is there a "right answer" to these kinds of questions? The answer is situational. For the wheat growers of Washington State where a foot of topsoil has disappeared in the last 40 years, the no-till method sounds pretty compelling. In a different landscape, ravaged by chemical pollution, the organic argument would probably win out.

When the Benefits Line Up

Of course, there are many situations where a clearer path exists. If all the stars align in a single direction, the choice is easy. For instance, the conference heard from dairy cooperative Organic Valley's Theresa Marquez about the benefits of their  approach: Organic farming creates richer and darker soil that is far better able to hold water and nutrients...organic cows fed a diet high in flaxseed oil produce more of the essential nutrient Omega-3 while decreasing the output of methane (a greenhouse gas linked even more heavily to global warming than carbon dioxide)—and they typically live up to three times longer than conventional-agriculture cows, which allows farms to be economically sustainable as well.

Marquez also noted that many of her member farms are planting some acreage in oilseed crops such as sunflowers, which can power a farm's trucks and tractors, feed its livestock and generate revenues.

The Challenges We Already Meet

Other speakers provided hope for meeting those difficult challenges mentioned earlier, by showing how their organizations are already surmounting equally difficult challenges. For example, Maisie Greenawalt of Bon Appetit Management Company (a food service provider to college, corporate, and organization cafeterias) inspired attenders with stories of converting institutional food service from slop to gourmet treats with fresh ingredients, and being profitable even while allowing college students unlimited trips to the (expensive, locally sourced, naturally raised non-antibiotic-treated beef) burger bar.

Not all sustainable food initiatives are local, of course. Fair trade— whose products often cross international borders—was also a much-discussed. From its beginnings in coffee, fair trade has olive oil, herbs, tea, cocoa, sugar, bananas,  and many others. Fair trade ensures that the farmer makes a decent livelihood and has good working conditions, and the fair trade movement is spreading into such areas as bridge loans for farmers who only get paid once a year.

And more and more companies are producing goods that are not only fairly traded but also organic, providing sustainability not only to the farmers but to consumers as well.

Big...Or Little?

While once the province of tiny little artisan firms, these products and processes are breaking out of their niches. More and more of the major players in the food industry are making shelf space or production line space for organic, natural, and fairly traded goods, and many of the smaller companies have been bought up by industry giants. While this came up frequently at the conference, questions about the roles of multinationals versus tiny independents will have to wait for another time.

Fukushima Accidents Make It Clear: **We Need Safe Energy Policies**, World-Wide

Among many environmentalists and politicians, even some who ought to know better, it's been an axiom that we need nuclear power, because coal is so dirty and toxic and contributes so heavily to climate heating.

Unfortunately, nuclear is also dirty and toxic, as well as extremely dangerous. And despite its claims, it's far from carbon-neutral when you look at the whole fuel cycle. Those who looked closely, long before the tsunami wrecked the Fukushima Daiichi six-reactor complex, have been opposing nuclear power for decades.

Problems with Nuclear

Here are just a few of the many severe problems with reliance on nuclear:

- ✓ If a plant has a major problem, and has to be removed from service permanently, it causes disruption in the energy systems of the communities that depend on it, because a lot of power generation is taken off the grid at once—and sinks enormous amounts of unrecoverable capital. In the case of Daiichi, most of those reactors can never be used again.

✓ The consequences of failure can be extremely severe (ask the people who used to live near Chernobyl, where a large swath of land remains uninhabitable after 25 years)—and the risk factors are numerous: not just earthquakes, tsunamis, hurricanes, and terrorism, but also component failure, and the lovely little thing called "human error" (both of which were factors in Fukushima, Chernobyl, and Three Mile Island).

✓ In many countries (including the United States, massive insurance subsidies and liability caps transfer almost all the risk from the utilities to ratepayers and area residents. If there's an accident don't expect to collect more than pennies on the dollar, if you get anything at all.

✓ Over the entire fuel cycle, starting with mining uranium and ending with attempting to find a solution for safe storage of nuclear waste, the process requires enormous energy inputs and excretes carbon, so the actual gains in usable power and greenhouse gas reduction are very tiny, if they exist at all. One study I've seen, by John J. Berger, states that from 1960-76, the nuclear power "generation" industry actually *consumed five times as much power as it generated.* I cited this study in my first book, Nuclear Lessons, published all the way back in 1980. For this, we're risking our future?

✓ And don't forget: there is no permanent solution to storage of radioactive waste, requiring isolation from the environment for up to a quarter of a million years. Considering that the oldest objects passed down to us are only about 40,000 years old, and that no human language has been around for even 5000 years, I have serious doubts about this.

Problems with Coal

OK, so what about coal?

- ✓ Just in the U.S., 104,722 coal mine workers were killed on the job in the past 110 years, an average of 952 deaths per year. In China, 2,433 miners were killed in 2010 alone.

- ✓ Much more sobering: in these two countries combined, a shocking 530,000 people reportedly die every year from coal-pollution-related diseases. Extrapolating worldwide, that means coal is responsible for millions of deaths per year. Clearly not sustainable.

The *Real* Alternatives

What, then, is the solution to our energy needs? It lies in the arms of good old Mother Nature.

Clean, renewable, non-destructive energy sources like solar, hydro, geothermal, wind, and even exotic sources like molecular or magnetic power can generate enough power so we can dispense with both coal and nuclear (as well as other polluting, greenhouse-gas-generating fuels like wood, which are renewable but not sustainable).

But in order to do so, we need to rethink the way we do energy. I propose three basic principles:

Energy should be generated close to or at the place where it will be used, to minimize friction and transmission losses.

Small-scale systems cause much fewer negative environmental consequences than large ones (for instance, in-river hydro that lets the water keep flowing is far more environmentally benign than large dams).

"Negawatts" and "negabarrels"—the energy we save by increasing our energy efficiency—can account for reductions of 50 percent or more in our energy needs.

So...how can we Green And Profitable entrepreneurs move this rethinking forward? For starters, we can make sure we've had recent energy audits at our businesses and homes, and have implemented many of the suggestions. We can look at  ways to conserve, and to use locally generated clean, renewable power. And we can create social pressure through our trade associations, our customer networks, and our purchasing to move away from every kind of unsustainable power source to the sustainable ones.

Sources:

Net loss of power from nuclear: Berger, John J. *Nuclear Power: The Univable Option* (New York: Dell, 1977, pp. 150-151, cited in Curtis, Richard, Elizabeth Hogan, Shel Horowitz. *Nuclear Lessons: An Examination of Nuclear Power's Safety, Economic, and Political Record* (Harrisburg: Stackpole, 1980, p. 90)

US coal mining fatalities: http://www.msha.gov/stats/centurystats/coalstats.asp

China coal mining fatalities: http://www.rfa.org/english/energy_watch/deaths-03072011114504.html

Coal pollution deaths in US and China: http://nextbigfuture.com/2008/03/deaths-per-twh-for-all-energy-sources.html

Energy savings from negawatts/negabarrels:
http://wn.com/amory_lovins_we_must_win_the_oil_endgame

The terms "negawatts" and "negabarrels" were popularized by physicist Amory Lovins, founder of he green energy think-tank Rocky Mountain Institute.

How to **Jumpstart** the **Renewable Economy** Worldwide

You may have read about the Marshall Plan, which restarted the economy of Europe following World War II.

With the threat of catastrophic climate change hovering over our heads, and with the economy still in tatters in many parts of the world, I suggest a worldwide Marshall Plan-style initiative. Let's stave off global warming, create jobs, put significant discretionary spending money into  the hands of citizens, and lower energy prices—all at no net cost to the taxpayers, property owners, and renters.

Strategies would include lowering the price of clean technology by increasing demand...making energy-saving technology accessible to low- and middle-income people (including renters), and using the money saved to spur sustainable economic development. The plan, which I'd hope would be adopted by national, regional, and local governments around the world, would have these components:

1. Effective immediately, starting with any plans proposed and not yet approved, all government or government-funded construction would be required to generate at least as much energy as it consumes, through clean and renewable technologies, such as solar, wind, small-scale hydro, magnetic, tidal, bacterial, and deep conservation (this is not a comprehensive list).

If compromise is necessary, aim for 10 percent or less energy consumption compared with traditional nongreen buildings serving the same purpose.

Technologies must be both clean and renewable, which means they cannot be based in fossil fuels, nuclear, or most types of biomass.

2. As prices come down due to increased demand and economies of scale, locally administered government programs make renewable and clean technologies available to people who can't afford them, but in ways that are financially self-supporting.

For example, governments and utilities can join forces to set up lease-back programs. The company that installs an alternative energy system maintains ownership, but leases the energy back to the homeowner or tenant. Or the government guarantees loans that enable homeowners to purchase the systems and automatically pay back the loans out of the energy savings.

3. The new government buildings save government agencies enormous amounts of money in utilities. Those savings are earmarked to retrofit existing government buildings.

4. As the private sector repays the loans or buys the leased energy, that money becomes available to retrofit nongovernment buildings

Large-scale implementation would bring down the price...make it affordable to every homeowner...reduce or eliminate dependence on foreign oil and uranium...reduce CO2 buildup and thus global warming. When, planet-wide, we see our rooftops as an energy (and possibly food) resource, and have programs in place to make these systems affordable to those without capital, we can eliminate oil dependence and reduce carbon emissions/global warming.

By outfitting every government building and providing means for low-income people to solarize, we can:

✓ Bring prices way down and make clean renewable energy more affordable to middle-income homeowners

✓ Free up capital currently spent on fossil fuels for economic development

✓ Create tens of thousands of new short-term jobs

✓ Reduce dependence on foreign oil

✓ Reduce pressure to "solve" our energy shortage through environmentally disastrous initiatives like tar-sands oil, fracking, and nuclear

✓ Slow or perhaps even reverse catastrophic climate change

We constantly hear dire predictions of what will happen if we don't address the carbon issue right away. Yet, even modest initiatives get caught in political wrangling and die a quick death. Because this program is essentially self-funding, and uses the workings of the free market to create affordable alternatives for the less wealthy, it should be politically easier to accomplish than other proposals—perhaps even in time to prevent climate catastrophe.

Meanwhile, the groundwork for this kind of international cooperation has already been laid. As one example, Put Solar On It <putsolaron.it>, an international initiative to get world leaders to solarize their presidential palaces, could be a natural organizing platform to expand from residences of heads of state to all government buildings. India, Chile, and the Maldives are among those who have already started solarizing their presidential palaces, and the U.S. could easily replace the solar panels that were installed on the White House all the way back in 1979 (unfortunately removed by the subsequent president). Expanding to the hundreds of thousands of other government buildings is a logical next step.

Let's show some initiative and gumption, put aside our cultural differences, and get this done.

Greenwashing,
Nuclear Power, and You

When I'm interviewed on radio, I'm almost invariably asked about greenwashing, and about being able to tell the difference between real green actions and fake ones.

Usually, I respond by citing the nuclear power industry as an example of how not to do green messaging.

Nuclear power's proponents claim it's a green technology, because spinning the turbines creates less carbon dioxide than spinning turbines using oil, coal, or natural gas. But that argument doesn't hold up to scrutiny; when you look at the entire cycle, from mining and milling the uranium through assembling it into nuclear fuel, transporting it across vast distances, loading it into the power plant, actually operating the plant, and then removing it afterwards, you find a significant carbon footprint (not to mention considerable consumption of energy).

And we don't even know the carbon impact of storing the waste long-term in complete isolation from the environment (we're talking about a quarter of a million years)—because the technology to do that doesn't even exist.

And then we've got the little matter of radiation. Dozens of isotopes are produced in the nuclear cycle, some of them not found in nature, and most of them highly toxic and carcinogenic.

This is all part of routine operation. When things go wrong, the negative environmental impact goes up by orders of magnitude. More than a quarter-century after the Chernobyl accident, vast areas of the Ukraine are still uninhabitable (including some parts that had been among the best farmland in Eastern Europe). And it's still not clear if a comparable disaster will occur at Fukushima-Dai'ichi, where the fuel rods from the #4 reactor are still in grave danger of catastrophic failure, and where at least two reactors melted down during the accident.

And if you think nuclear accidents only happen once in a long while, consider this: We've heard about Three Mile Island, Chernobyl, and now, the second (2011) major failures at Fukushima. But those are only the most publicized in a long line of accidents at nuclear power plants and related facilities. From 1952 to 2009, there were at least 99 accidents causing loss of life or at least USD $50,000 in property damage, and that does not count the Fukushima accidents in 2010 and 2011.

Chernobyl alone, according to European reports, has caused a shocking 1 million deaths and $500,000,000,000 in property damage—and that's before long-latency cancers start to show up.

I wouldn't call that green!

So what does this mean for those of us in the green marketing world?

First, we have an obligation to protect our industry by confronting this falsehood. As some countries are drawing away from nuclear power, others (including the US) still embrace it. We need to use the full weight of our marketing skills to get the message out that nuclear is the most ungreen technology ever created, that it is not a solution. And that we have plenty of solutions that are appropriate, using renewable, nonpolluting, safe technologies such as human-scale solar, wind, hydro, tidal, and geothermal.

Second and even more importantly, we have an obligation to our planet to protect ourselves from this menace. Whenever new nuclear power (or renewal of existing nuclear power) is proposed, we need to be there opposing it, demonstrating not only the greenwashing lies but the cost to our health, safety, and even our freedom.

If you'd like to know more, I'll send you the ten-page update I wrote when my 1980 book was reprinted in Japan, post-Fukushima (which includes reference citations). Please write to me, shel AT greenandprofitable.com, with the subject line "Send 2011 Nuke Intro."

Shifting to a
Global
Perspective

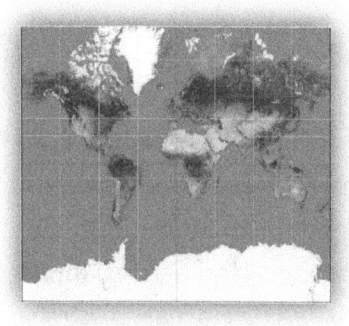

As a child growing up in the United States of the 1960s and 1970s, I knew only one map of the world: the Mercator projection that makes the polar regions look bigger, and the equatorial areas smaller, than their actual relative sizes. Usually, the Americas were in the center with eastern Asia and Australia on the left—and Europe, Africa, and western Asia on the right; once in a while, I'd see a version that put Europe and Africa in the center, Asia connected to it on the right, and Greenland and the Americas across the Atlantic to the left—the version that most European students my age and older grew up with.

In these maps, Greenland appears to be bigger than Australia and India combined; Greenland actually appears to be larger than Africa. In reality, Africa, at 30,065,000 sq km (11,608,161.4 square miles), is 14 times the size of Greenland.

It's impossible to accurately project a round sphere like the earth onto a rectangle. Something has to give. In Mercator projections, the shapes of land masses are pretty accurate—but the sizes are wildly distorted.

But in the Peters projection developed much later (in 1974), those distortions are reversed. Land masses show their relative size, but the shapes are barely recognizable. The first time I saw a Peters map,

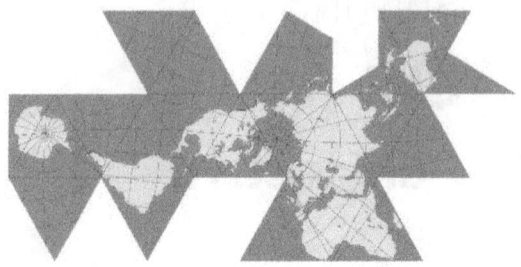 probably about 30 years ago, it was a shock. It changed the way I think about the world.

And I love Buckminster Fuller's Dymaxion Map, centered on the North Pole, which keeps both sizes and shapes of landmasses accurate, but does very strange things to the distances between continents. In Fuller's map, the world's land masses appear as a nearly-connected chain, surrounded by a single ocean. Australia, Eurasia, and Africa show deep commonalities of interest, while North America appears as close to Europe as to South America.

Dymaxion, Peters and Mercator are only three of a wide range of global maps. You can make a map that has the top in any direction; here, for instance, are several with south at the top, giving prominence to South America, southern Africa, and Australia: flourish.org/upsidedownmap

And since the Earth is a sphere, you can also make a map with the center at any point you like; I've seen various maps with Toronto, Tokyo, and Mecca at the center.

So, you ask—what on Earth does this have to do with profitable green business? Quite a bit, actually.

✓ How we map the world influences our worldview.

For European and North American explorers and conquerors, growing up with a view of Africa as smaller than Greenland perhaps made it easier to minimize the many accomplishments of African cultures, dehumanize the dark-skinned people of Africa as inferior—and then intellectually justify the history of imperialism and exploitation that followed.

In today's multicultural world, understanding the importance of the Global South helps us remember that, for example, we can't just ship off our toxic byproducts and bury them in some developing country.

- ✓ The creativity of these different maps and the thousands of other variations reminds us that sometimes, simple answers to complex problems such as environmental devastation are a lot easier to see if we shift our perspective (as we talked about in last month's column on simple elegance).

- ✓ Maps can show much more than position.

"Heat map"-style infographics can show relative accomplishments, population, natural resources and other factors—and green entrepreneurs can use these as planning tools that take environmental and social factors into consideration

In short, maps, as windows on the natural and the human-created worlds, serve different purposes. Mercator was a very appropriate choice for 17th- and 18th-century sailors wanting the easiest transit between Europe and North America, while Dymaxion is perfect to bring home Fuller's concept of "Spaceship Earth"—an interconnected single ecosystem.

For a detailed and fascinating look at how maps shape our thinking, I strongly recommend **Seeing Through Maps: Many Ways to See the World**, by Denis Wood, Ward L. Kaiser, and Bob Abramms, ODTMaps.com/detail.asp_Q_product_id_E_STM-2-BKttty

How to **Influence** Public Officials on **Environmental Issues**

As both a marketing consultant and environmental activist, I'm accustomed to writing or presenting words that convince the public to change their positions—or their brands—and to take action based on my writing or speaking.

To do this, I will use my powers of persuasion and a wide range of language aimed at moving different types of people forward toward a common agenda. My arguments will typically be a mix of emotion and intellect, of appeals to self-interest and appeals to the common good.

But I've learned over the years that when the goal is influencing public officials, the rules and strategies are different.

For one thing, when government officials take testimony on an issue, they typically have a very narrow scope. In fact, they're often not even allowed to consider anything outside their purview (this is one of the reasons why change involving action by government enforcement agencies or getting new laws passed can be frustratingly slow). So big, sweeping appeals along broad issues have little effect.

Last month, I wanted to weigh in before a government body on one of those big-picture issues. I submitted testimony to a state government agency on whether it should issue a certain permit to a nuclear power plant. I wanted to address the much wider issue of nuclear power plant safety—but I had to do it within the narrow confines of what the board could address.

I think my testimony makes an instructive example of how to influence governments—so let me point out a few things about my testimony
(which I've posted at shelhorowitz.com/go/nucleartestimony):

- ✓ Establish credentials—why it's your right to give testimony.

Right at the beginning, I note that I've written three relevant books— and this is especially important since I'm not a resident of the state where the plant is located. Credentials don't have to be formal, though. Yours might be "resident within the evacuation zone" or "parent of a special-needs child."

- ✓ Focus on the issue the agency can act on.

The hearing was about whether the state should grant the nuke a new Certificate of Public Good. So very early, I looked at what it means to provide public good—and then I referred back to this concept several times, including the last sentence.

- ✓ Use an objective-sounding, intelligent tone.

Not the time for screaming hype or unsubstantiated accusations.

- ✓ Respect their knowledge and intelligence.

Notice that I didn't explain the Price-Anderson Act; I simply referenced it with an "as you know."

✓ Provide a framework for addressing the wider issues.

By US federal law, the federal Nuclear Regulatory Commission has jurisdiction over the safety of nuclear power plants. But the state of Vermont can take economic factors into account when evaluating whether the plant serves a public good—so I anchored all my safety arguments in their impact on the state's economy and overtly stated that this is why I was bringing up the safety issues.

✓ Back up your claims and cite sources.

I cite three books, the plant's own accident report, one third-party scientific report, and two top-tier newspaper articles (from the New York Times and Washington Post).

✓ Clearly state the desired action the agency should take, ideally quite early in your remarks.

In this case, I want the Public Service Board to deny the Certificate of Pubic Good requested by Entergy, and I say so very specifically in the second sentence: "Like the majority of people who have come before you to testify, I ask that you deny the Certificate of Public Good for Entergy for the continued operation of the Vermont Yankee nuclear power plant."

✓ Use "social proof"—demonstrate that lots of people agree with you.

Look again at the quote from my testimony in the previous paragraph: the first half of the sentence is all about social proof; the second half tells them what I want them to do.

- ✓ Be organized ahead of time, and be conscious of time limits if speaking in person, and be willing to provide your full, extended testimony in writing.

I had an outline with me of points I could make within two minutes. It would not have been nearly as complete, but it would have hit the important points.

For maximum impact, make copies of your statement available to the media and to the public. My statement is published on my website, and thus my potential audience is a lot bigger than the three members of the Public Service Board.

Green Advocates Must **Convince** the Other Side **with Economic Arguments**

Last month, one town away from me, there was a big dustup when the city decided to spray some athletic fields with Roundup. In addition to concerns about the health effects on the children who'd be playing on those fields, the parcel happens to directly about a commercial organic farm—one about to receive USDA organic certification, which means that it's been chemical-free for three years.

I sent a letter to the Mayor, selected members of the City Council, the Recreation Department, and the Chair of the Board of Public Works. I also copied a reporter at the local paper.

I'm going to share the relevant portions of that e-mail with you, then discuss why I framed it as I did—because there are many lessons in advocacy here, not only in the public sphere, but in dealing with any stakeholders on sustainability issues:

As a customer of Crimson & Clover Farm and many other organic farms in the area...a 26-1/2-year property owner in Northampton (through this past April), and an internationally recognized expert in the marketing of green products and services, I urge you in the strongest possible terms to BLOCK the proposed spraying of Roundup.

You are no doubt aware of the growing importance of agritourism and ecotourism in Northampton and the Pioneer Valley—which includes at least two lodging establishments within the City that specifically cater to a green clientele (Starlight Lama and Trailside B&Bs). Much in that sector has to do with a creating and sustaining a culture of support for local organic foods that includes both farmers and consumers. I even use the Valley as an example in my speaking and writing on green business, nationally and internationally.

—> Spraying Roundup—a pesticide whose long-term safety is highly questionable—could have severe deleterious effects on Crimson & Clover and Grow Food Northampton.

Spraying could easily drift onto the wrong fields and/or contaminate nearby water, resulting in a loss of Crimson & Clover's organic certification, a loss of customers—I am one who would not knowingly buy from a farm tainted by Roundup—and *possible lawsuits* for interfering with the livelihood of another.

And did you know that in addition to selling Roundup, Monsanto sells Roundup-tolerant GMO seeds, and then sues farmers whose fields get contaminated with them for using the seeds without permission? I have a lot of trouble with their ethics. Roundup furthers Monsanto's actions to crush local and organic agriculture...

Meanwhile, I hope you will use your influence to prevent this potential can of worms from ever being opened—and I hope to greet the three of you at the rally at Crimson & Clover tomorrow afternoon.

Why This Approach?

Paragraph 1: Establishing my credentials.

I am affected by what affects this farm, because I am a customer. I owned a home in that town for a long period of time. And I happen to have validated expertise in the subject. But if you don't have textbook credentials, you can work with what you have. For instance, you could speak as a property owner, parent, and purchaser of organic foods.

Paragraph 2: Identifying organic agriculture as an important and growing sector in the local economy.

This is critical; organic agriculture is too often seen as marginal and trivial. I shown that tax-paying businesses are affected by the city's decision—and that the region has been a model for the rest of the country and even the world.

Paragraphs 3 and 4: Demonstrating the potential negative economic consequences to the affected business, *and* to the city.

All municipalities in my area are strapped for cash. This city even went through a very contentious vote to raise taxes just a few months ago, to avoid severe layoffs across many departments.

Avoiding adding to that burden with preventable lawsuits is an argument to make the government pay attention.

Paragraph 5: The wider context.

In my writing and speaking, I often talk about combining self-interest and planetary interest messages. This is the planetary part. Monsanto's frequent legal challenges to farmers whose fields were contaminated by drift is a serious problem in the organic farming world.

Paragraph 6: Offering a positive step.

I conclude the letter with something these officials can do to show their solidarity and gain public support.

Results: One City Councilor did attend the rally. And the Mayor announced a compromise plan that put a no-spray buffer around the edge. Without the buffer on city land, the organic farm would have had to sacrifice three acres for its own buffer in order to obtain that organic certification. While it wasn't the ideal outcome, it was much better than the original plan, and shows the power of organizing along economic interest.

Polarization vs. **Unification**

Is polarization an effective strategy for change?

I've felt for decades that confronting the power structure—and shaking up the "truths" that people might hold dear—is essential to creating the better world we all seek.

But by itself, that isn't enough. Yes, if you want to accomplish deep change, you need polarizers to create awareness and shake up the status quo—and you also need unifiers to put the shattered pieces back together and facilitate forward movement. Without both halves, the yin and the yang of organizing, very little actually changes, either in the business world or in the streets.

I've played both roles at various times. For about the last 20 years, I've been much more about creating unity and moving the larger world to social change—in many cases, using business to enable that change.

Years earlier, I'd been a polarizer. I remember a conversation in early 1976, when I was 19. I don't remember what I'd said, but my listener, probably 20 years older than me, turned to me and asked, "Why are you so bitter?"

I'd never thought of myself as bitter. Angry, certainly. The Vietnam war had been raging until the previous year. My government had been killing or jailing many agents of social change. The business community seemed a heartless, soulless place that cared only for profits—I've obviously learned a different truth since then—and the environment was visibly in jeopardy. The more we worked for a better world, the farther away it seemed.

Yet, even then, I had at least a bit of hope—but apparently, I wasn't very good at conveying that hope. I have a whole lot more hope now than I did 38 years ago. Maybe that's why lately I've been much more drawn to building consensuses than to shattering doctrines.

I believe that we make change by harnessing those opposites into something greater than either part. Perhaps you need the doom-and-gloom alarmism of people like anti-nuclear activist Dr. Helen Caldicott of Australia or suburbia-is-dying prophet James Kunstler of

the United States before people will respond to the optimism of people like energy futurist Amory Lovins and the late bacterial scholar Lynn Margulis. Perhaps you need the loud unkempt rebels of the Occupy movement to hear the quiet voices of Israeli and Palestinian families joining hands in mutual condolence and holding a banner together for peace.

Yes, we need to know the terrible consequences of nonaction, of allowing a planet in crisis to deepen that crisis. But if we're going to move out of that crisis, that needs a platform too. Before people reach the depth of despair, extend the hand up they need to get back into turning the existing into the possible, and the possible into the amazing.

In every aspect of modern life—energy, agriculture, transportation, construction, waste reduction, to name just a few—brilliant minds are at work solving all those huge problems. We know so much more about all of this than we used to know.

Those advances are everywhere you look in the green world. Think about the order-of-magnitude increase in the efficiency of comparably priced photovoltaic panels just in the past ten years. Think about organic agriculture—  not only vastly more productive, but producing food that looks better and tastes better, and using new models of distribution such as Community Supported Agriculture. Think about Zero waste, making gains in using every resource more efficiently. And most of all, think of how the environmental movement has shifted the consciousness of ordinary people around the world—think of the impact that you've had, in your own work.

Could those gains have been accomplished while swimming in a cold sea of negativity, fatalism, and beating ourselves up for killing the world? No; in a climate that drives away optimism and hope, depression leads to paralysis. But could those gains have been accomplished in a Polyanna climate of nothing's ever wrong? No, again; there would be no incentive to improve.

Let's end this business column with a business example. 30 years ago, I got my first computer, an original 128K Apple Macintosh. A major advance in both computing power and usability, this state-of-the-art machine had just 128 kilobytes—not megabytes and certainly not gigabytes—of memory (twice what the IBM PC had at the time). It had no hard drive, just a single 400K disk drive. The tiny 9-inch (22.86 cm) display was black-and-white. To get online, I dialed up over a 300 bps modem and watched my text-only characters pour

slowly across the screen and into cyberspace. That machine, less powerful than any smart phone today, cost $3000 US.

Today, Apple is mainstream. But it's worth remembering that the Macintosh was quite deliberately polarizing. In the very first ad, a runner smashed a dictator's video monitor with a hammer. The later Mac vs. PC series continued the theme. Yet, the original Macintosh motto was the uniting "computer for the rest of us," and the company's greatest successes were built on very inclusive, ground-breaking, problem-solving products aimed squarely at the mainstream: the iPod, iPhone, and iPad.

Which role does your business play right now?

Sustainability is **Not** Enough

In the green world, we hear the terms sustainable or sustainability quite often. Sustainability is a good first step. But is that really all we want?

Not even close. Sustainability means making sure the status quo—the existing situation—can self-replicate. But keeping the current situation from getting worse doesn't mean it's getting better.

Experts put the safe level of carbon in the atmosphere at 350 parts per million. But the August 2014 figure was 397.01 parts per million, or 113 percent of what it should be. And it's probably not a coincidence that extreme weather events (floods, droughts, intense hurricanes, tsunamis, tornados, and such) have become both a lot more common and much more catastrophic.

The 14 years of the 21st century have included nine of the ten warmest years in the past 134 years; the sole 20th-century year in the hottest ten was 1998—almost into the 21st.

Our non-renewable resources are being depleted. Whether it's oil (used not only for energy but for most plastics), iron ore, bauxite (raw material for aluminum), or the rare-earth metals used to make products like cell phones, the raw materials that were highest quality and easiest to extract have already been harvested. The remaining materials are harder to extract, require more energy to process, and/or generate more pollution. Energy extraction methods like tar sands oil or fracking can wreak environmental devastation. Tar sands oil is dirty and low quality, scars the landscape, and requires enormous energy input. Fracking is more efficient and actually cheaper than the old methods, but puts our water supplies—our most precious resource—at risk. "Mountaintop removal" destroys whole ecosystems to get coal out of the ground.

Products and their components—even food—travel thousands of unnecessary miles. The deck seems stacked against truly local economies.

Our world takes enormous unnecessary risks by disregarding the Precautionary Principle and unleashing technologies whose effects are not known—like GMO foods—or that are known to be

potentially catastrophic—like nuclear power—because we use narrow cost-benefit analyses that only selectively count costs and disregard the complexities of lifecycles and disposal.

We want a world that's getting better. We want a world that's undoing the damage humans have caused to the planet. And I think it's safe to say that as green business owners, we want to be part of that healing.

So let's reframe the conversation. Let's stop talking about sustainability—and start talking in terms like "regeneration" and "restoration."

And let's create structures that empower businesses to combine the vision of what needs to change with the commitment to change it. Alternative business structures, from B-corporations to coops, are a first step. But beyond that, let's harness the profit motive to *get it done.*

In 2014, we should no longer put up with a world full of misery. Isn't it time to reward businesses that are working meaningfully to end hunger, poverty, war, and climate catastrophe while penalizing those that are stuck in the rapacious practices of the past?

I've expanded on some of these ideas in a 15-minute TED talk, "Impossible is a Dare: Business For a Better World." Please watch it (and see the slides) at; www.business-for-a-better-world.com/tedtalks

And please visit http://business-for-a-better-world.com, where you'll find the beginnings of resources to address and *solve* these issues, including the chance to nominate your favorite socially conscious business project so others can work on it too.

Source for August 2014 carbon level and hottest years: http://co2now.org/

* * *

I enjoyed writing this column from 2010 to 2014, and I think I provided very high value for those who read it. Unfortunately, I never got enough markets to make the project economically viable.

As I move in the direction of helping companies see the value in solving problems like hunger, poverty, war, and climate catastrophe, I can no longer afford the luxury of doing this column for the few markets that subscribed. So this will be the last issue for a while.

I'd love to bring it back, if I can get to a minimum number of subscribers each paying just $10 per month. If you have possible markets for me, please drop me a line at shel AT greenandprofitable.com with the subject "Column Market."

Disclaimer: The very observant among you may notice that some examples come up more than once. Keep in mind that this ebook is a compilation of a monthly column that ran for four years. I have organized the columns by topic rather than chronologically here, and as a result, columns that may have been years apart end up close to each other in the same ebook. Yes, some examples are repeated, but they were inserted to make different points, at different times. Please also note that nothing in this ebook series should be taken as legal or professional advice, and as in any situation, your results may vary as you implement the tips and ideas.

About Shel Horowitz and
Business For a Better World

Green business profitability expert Shel Horowitz shows businesses how to profit both by going green and by addressing problems like hunger and poverty, war, violence, and catastrophic climate change. Active in both marketing and the environment since his teen years in the early 1970s, Shel is the award-winning author of eight books including long-running Amazon category bestseller *Guerrilla Marketing Goes Green*.

- ✓ As a consultant, Shel brings laser focus to turning problems into opportunities, opening new markets, and helping you identify potential partners.

- ✓ As a marketing and informational copywriter trained in journalism, Shel is known for his clear writing, ability to make technical concepts accessible, and his skill in telling "the story behind the story" to move people to action.

- ✓ As an international speaker and trainer, Shel combines dynamic vocal style with powerful graphics and gets his audiences actively involved. He's spoken at major business and environmental conferences in locations as diverse as Istanbul, Davos (Switzerland), and Honolulu.

After over a decade actively assisting green businesses with their marketing, Shel branched out in 2014 to help businesses seize profit opportunities in turning hunger and poverty into sufficiency, war and violence into peace, and catastrophic climate change into planetary balance—and helping individuals reclaim their power to actively create this better world.

Shel is happy to talk to you about helping in any of these areas. Reach him at 413-586-2388 (8 a.m. to 10 p.m. US Eastern Time), email shel AT greenandprofitable.com, or find him on Twitter @ShelHorowitz.

Shel also has a gift for you: a free copy of his ebook, *Painless Green: 111 Tips to Help the Environment, Lower Your Carbon Footprint, Cut Your Budget, and Improve Your Quality of Life—With No Negative Impact on Your Lifestyle*. To claim your free copy of this $9.95 ebook, visit PainlessGreenBook.com/earthday and use the code, G&Pebook.

One more set of gifts, FREE with your no-cost subscription to Shel Horowitz's monthly Clean and Green Newsletter:

- ✓ Seven Tips to Gain Marketing Traction as a Green Guerrilla

- ✓ Seven Weeks to a Greener Business: once a week for seven weeks, tips on going greener with printing, energy saving, waste reduction, water conservation, transportation, going deep-green, and of course, green marketing.

- ✓ Plus the informative monthly newsletter, published since 1997 and featuring a business tip or profile plus a book review each issue.

Sign up in the upper-right-hand corner at http://greenandprofitable.com.

Green and
Profitable

BOOK 4

The New Realities of
21st Century Business

Shel Horowitz

Can One Community
Self-Sufficiency Initiative
Really Do All This?

What if a single action could: get troubled teens off the streets and into something productive—and develop their entrepreneurship skills in the process...provide fresh local organic food to inner-city people with no other access to quality produce...clean up a blighted neighborhood vacant lot and spark a caring community spirit? What if that action could be done without any significant government or corporate resources, other than a space to have it?

Sound like a lot to do at once? Oddly enough, it's probably easier to create a single action that accomplishes multiple goods than to create a program that requires massive intravenous injections of outside aid to address only one of  those goals. (And this is a sustainability principle that's true in many areas: energy, transportation, manufacturing, and more.)

This particular set of objectives can all be met by creating urban community gardens, and any business owner can benefit by facilitating their creation. Your own property values go up, risk of crime and vandalism goes down, and you add to your standing in your home community.

All you need to do is find some neighborhood leaders who'll get the project going, and provide a quarter-acre or so of unused land (ideally, a parcel that can be expanded as the project succeeds)—or even an appropriately engineered rooftop.

Successes are happening all over the country.[2] A few among many:

- ✓ 25 kids, ages 9-17, run the Brightmoor Youth Garden on Detroit's west side, start to finish. Last year, they planted, maintained, harvested and sold 1,300 pounds—$2,700 worth of—produce. And this is only one of numerous local food projects in Detroit.[3]

- ✓ In Richmond, California (near San Francisco), a community group called Urban Tilth has two farms based at schools and is planning to hire 26 kids to plant and manage an

[2] The author thanks Johanna Halbeisen of Good News Radio for bringing several of these stories to his attention.

[3] http://www.detnews.com/article/20100811/OPINION03/8110347/1448/LIFESTYL E14/Detroit-community-gardens-grow-optimism

orchard. One of these farms involves 30 students in a class called "Urban Ecology and Food Systems," whose curriculum integrates lessons from the garden into the classroom.[4]

✓ The city of Cleveland, hit hard by the recession, has 3,300 acres of vacant land and 15,000 vacant buildings within city limits. Rather than blast big swaths through the neighborhoods in the traditional urban renewal "solutions," the city is reclaiming 15 parcels in a pilot project to grow its own food—adding to the 175 community gardens and 40 for-profit market gardens already in existence. Bobbi Reichtell, senior vice president for programs of Neighborhood Progress Inc. (the group coordinating the effort) has an ambitious goal: returning $800 million a year to the local economy by raising the percentage of locally grown food in Cleveland from 2 percent to 10 percent.[5]

✓ Nuestras Raices, a longstanding community group in depressed Holyoke, Massachusetts, has started an urban farm and several spin-off businesses. As its farmers gain skills in the business world, the organization helps them start mini-farms of

[4] http://www.yesmagazine.org/issues/a-resilient-community/from-vacant-city-lots-to-food-on-the-table
[5] http://www.cityfarmer.info/2010/05/10/from-vacant-to-vibrant-re-imagining-cleveland/

their own, and new farmers take their place on the original land.[6] Interestingly enough, Nuestras Raices itself was founded by a group of community gardeners.

✓ In Portland, Oregon, 3000 residents work the city's community gardens, and another 1000 are on a waiting list.[7]

✓ On the rooftops of the neighborhood once written off as "Fort Apache," Sustainable South Bronx is growing food, extending the lives of the buildings, and slashing energy use.[8]

If this multiplicity of benefits could make a huge difference in your community, consider helping one get started. Maybe your corporate headquarters has a sunny section of lawn that could become garden space (and perhaps reduce the health risks to your employees from pesticide use)—or your retail location has an unused roof. Do you happen to have a skilled gardener on staff who'd like to volunteer a few hours to train neighborhood kids and get the project going? Can such an initiative tie in to zero-waste, buy-local or other green projects you're already doing?

And can *you* benefit by branding your firm in your community as an advocate for jobs, entrepreneurship, improving the environment, healthy fresh food, and re-skilling our youth?

---

[6] http://www.nuestras-raices.org/en/nuestras-raices-farm
[7] http://www.yesmagazine.org/issues/food-for-everyone/fresh-from-...-the-city
[8] http://www.ssbx.org/index.php?link=31

Asking for Help
from the **Cloud Crowd**

Compare the before- and after-versions of this three-minute video promoting my "Making Green Sexy" speech:

BEFORE: youtu.be/FtghtR8lcrY

AFTER: youtu.be/DByWN4Feaj0

How did I know how to improve it? I asked on the cloud.

For nearly 20 years, when I want feedback on an idea or a project, help choosing book covers or titles, or recommendations on service providers, one of the places I turn to is the cloud. It's certainly not the only place I go for feedback and advice—but consistently, I get very useful help.

I started participating in online discussion groups in 1994, back when the only groups I'd experienced online were discussion boards on AOL. By 1995, I was exploring online groups on the wider Internet.

Over the years, I've joined dozens. Often, I unsubscribe again within a few months or a couple of years. But there are groups I participate in that I've been involved with since the 20th century. Some of these are organized by industry (green marketing, book publishing, speaking, etc.), some are general business discussion lists. Some are moderated (where an administrator has to approve each post); some are open.

Advice quality will vary. Often, there will be a mixture of great and terrible, and it's up to you to sort the difference.

And that's one of the reasons why it helps to participate actively on a list for a while before asking for this kind of help. First, this makes you a known quantity, someone who has helped others and therefore incites others to reciprocate when you need help; you'll get more, and better, responses. And second, it gives you the judgment to recognize who knows what they're talking about and who's just winging it.

It was a publishing group, years ago, that convinced me not to go to press with the title "Win-Win Marketing." I had asked for help choosing between two subtitles, and was told by several people I respect that my main title had implications I  didn't want. It took two months to come up with the right title for that book, which finally went to press as "Principled Profit: Marketing That Puts People First"—a much better title. (Ironically enough, the book's Spanish-language publisher in Mexico—without ever knowing about its almost-title—dubbed it "Mercadotechnia Basada en Ganar-Ganar," which literally translates as "Marketing Based in Win-Win." Maybe the same negative baggage doesn't apply in Mexican culture.)

For feedback on the speaker video, I posted to several discussion lists on green business, general marketing, and local business in my area. I got far and away the most useful (and the largest number of) comments from a LinkedIn discussion group called "Step Into the Spotlight," where I happen to be quite active. I received several public and a few private responses that were quite helpful.

Responses broke down in to three categories:

- ✓ Suggested improvements that were useful and easy to implement

- ✓ Suggested improvements that would improve the video but would be too hard to implement because I didn't have the right footage available

- ✓ Suggestions I did not feel would improve the video

Among the advice I accepted: move the 33% ROI bit higher, get rid of some of the slow parts, insert some audience shots (my video producer found only one usable one in all my footage), rerecord the voiceovers around the two endorsements and cut down the verbiage on those slides, drop some of my narrative in places, and fix an audio quality issue in one section that I hadn't even noticed.

Suggestions I'd have liked to do couldn't easily enough: reducing the number of times I blink (my eyes are very sensitive to environmental irritants, and I blink a lot)—and fixing a word order issue that would have required replacing actual audio from one of my speeches with a new recording.

One of the suggestions I rejected entirely was that audiences can't handle the idea of three different types of audiences for green products and services. I disagree; in fact, I would not feel I delivered value if I spent a whole 60- or 90-minute speech making just one or two points. I don't want people in the audience to feel like they've been hit by a water cannon, but at the same time, I want them to come away feeling they know more, understand more, and have multiple tools in their own tool boxes that they can implement in their own marketing.

Once again, this sort of informal focus group proved its worth to me. In my mind, the later version is a vast improvement.

Next month: how to use these types of discussion lists to grow your business.

Look **Outside Your Box**: What Can Other Industries and Other Environments **Teach You About Synergy**

Would you believe a powerful green business was inspired by the space program? Believe it.

Swedish entrepreneur Mehrdad Mahdjoubi thought about how little water astronauts use in space and how much of their water gets recycled; he wondered why we couldn't adapt that water use pattern to our own households.

The result? The OrbSys: A shower that uses only 3 percent of the water and 20 percent of the energy of a typical shower, while claiming to produce higher comfort and better sanitation (note the appeal on multiple benefits). Mahdjoubi claims typical users could save $1000 per year.

By recycling most of the water, much less is needed. But the extra benefit was that much less energy is required as well, *because the water going back into the showerhead is already hot from its first pass.* If you've ever stood to the side as a whole lot of cold water came out of the showerhead before it was warm enough to step under, you know exactly why this is important. (Read more about Mahdjoubi and the OrbSys at http://ow.ly/ruUW2 and many other places; he's good at getting publicity.)

Remember this, too: the first or even the second categories of drive-through businesses weren't restaurants; they were banks, starting in 1930, and car washes, beginning later that decade. Some smart person looked outside the box and thought, "if people appreciate being able to bank from their cars, maybe they'd like to get their food handed to them in their cars, too." And by 1948, there was at least one drive-through eatery. Since then, the model has spread to other industries as well, including dry-cleaners and at least one wedding chapel.

While drive-through businesses aren't particularly eco-friendly, it's easy to find other examples within the green world.

Think about the spiral of creativity that started with shopping carts. Inventor Sylvan Goldman was inspired to create the first in-store shopping cart (patented in 1937) by looking at a folding chair (itself a wonderful space-saving, and thus green, invention). Someone else studied his invention and figured out  that a version shoppers could take home would be very helpful for urban dwellers who might not be able to park right next to their house (or might not own a car).

Someone else thought about substituting bicycles for delivery trucks, perhaps after watching a shopper pull a cart through a crowded street while cars and trucks were stuck in traffic. Someone else discovered bicycles could be adapted for other industrial uses, even trash hauling. All of these innovations reduce the number of car and truck trips. And that makes them green.

Another great green example is the whole phenomenon of upcycling: turning waste materials into consumer products. Think about the leap of consciousness to see a bunch of old computer chips, vinyl records, or bicycle parts (to name three popular raw materials used in upcycling)  and imagine them as works of art, or home decor, or home furnishings, or jewelry, or clothing. My daughter's purse and my wallet used to be automobile tires. We own a couple of tote bags that had past lives as plastic soda bottles. Recycled, repurposed material shows up in kitchen counters, decking and fencing, building materials, clothing, garden aids, and all sorts of other places.

In short, as a culture, we have begun to learn to ask the key question: "now that I'm done with the original purpose, what else can this be used for?"

Of course, this is not a new conversation—there's a decades-old expression: "Use it up, wear it out, make it do or do without," and a long and honorable tradition of repurposing extending to every area of life, even musical instruments made of old oil drums. But what's different is that upcycling has become mainstream. Repurposing is no longer just for frugality geeks or environmental activists; it has even penetrated the elegant boutiques that cater to fashion-conscious upscale consumers. Yes, green is now chic. Recycled and upcycled products are "in" now.

And you as a green business owner should be paying careful attention to this trend, and how it can benefit your business.

A Pessimist and an **Optimist**

Just as I was pondering what to write about in this month's column, I went to a pair of lectures organized by Nerd Nite Northampton (yep—that's how they spell it).

The juxtaposition of the two talks was striking. I don't know if the organizers considered this aspect—but one was very optimistic, and the other quite pessimistic about living here on Planet Earth.

The optimist, photojournalist Greg Saulmon, took us on a tour of the amazing birds of urban, industrial Holyoke and Springfield, Massachusetts: snowy owls, spotted owls, Cooper's and redtail hawks, bald eagles, peregrine falcons, and a host of smaller birds. His stunning photography captured a pair of raptors on the roof of an

industrial building, framed by a plume of steam. He caught birds doing acrobatics and birds speeding through the air. Birds on building gutters and an owl in the back yard of a woman who thanked him for being in the news media and wanting to report something other than a shooting.

His message was simple: nature is all around us, even in cities—and our kids can learn to love it. We can create effective habitat for both wild animals and people, even in the toughest inner-city neighborhoods.

As a New York City native, I concur. Watching Saulmon's talk, "The Birds Downtown," I kept thinking about my own childhood in a far more urban place than Holyoke, and how much nature I experienced even in one of the largest cities in the country.

Many of my earliest encounters with nature were within the city limits—in the parks and on the beaches, of course—but also in the plane trees that lined many city streets (dwarfed though they were by the giant buildings around them), and the little oases of parkland. Noticing the different grasses growing along an abandoned railroad track, tromping through city parks with my high school biology teacher as he led a tree identification walk, observing squirrels, and even going hawk-watching with my mom at the Pelham Bay Landfill, just a mile from our 20th floor apartment in a 26-storey high-rise, part of a complex of 33 high-rise apartment buildings tucked into a corner of the Bronx.

This neighborhood of 58,000 people was not important enough to get a subway extension, or even to make a new station on the commuter rail line that bordered the project. But while it may not have gotten on the radar of city planners, it definitely did get on the radar of the migrating birds. The buildings were spaced some distance apart from each other, and there was a lot of open land. Active marshlands bordered the community, and the Hutchinson River and Long Island Sound lay just beyond. A resident colony of geese acted like they owned the place, and gulls were always swooping around.

So if you live in a city—help your kids, or the kids who live near you appreciate nature. The first step in saving the world is awareness, and you can be part of that.

The second talk of the evening was much less upbeat. Filmmaker Ian Cheney's "The End of Darkness" focused on a part of nature that's slipping away rapidly: a night sky dark enough to see thousands of stars.

Growing up in New York City, there was so much light pollution that I never knew what the sky is supposed to look like. Cheney described a New York City native who thought the Hayden Planetarium sky show was a hoax. And I can understand that,  because when I used to walk home from the subway at night—a mile walk along an eight-lane highway—I'd never seen more stars than I could count—usually few enough that I could actually count them on my fingers. And living in a rural area for many years now, I'm still amazed when I look up on a clear night and see thousands of little dots of light.

But star deprivation, says Cheney, isn't just an aesthetic issue; it has severe consequences for our own and other species. Two among several examples: 1. Sea turtle hatchlings have evolved to head toward the brightest thing they see when they emerge at night from their eggs—because, historically, the ocean, catching the moonlight in its water, was brighter than the land. But now, if their mothers bury the eggs near a coastal city like Miami, the turtle babies head downtown, and die before they find the ocean.

The human example is even more disturbing; there seems to be a correlation between the false daylight of our populated areas—and breast cancer. Cheney doesn't have a solution—but he knows we need to look at this as a society.

Failure is **Always** an Option

I laugh whenever I hear that famous phrase, "failure is not an option." It shows not only enormous ignorance of the real world and the human brain, but also enormous hubris.

Let's get real. Failure is always an option—with sufficient bad luck or timing, loss of motivation, key player defections, or inadequate funding. This doesn't mean the task is impossible; it's just that currently, for whatever reason, it doesn't seem worth marshaling the necessary resources to finish the task.

Sometimes, we can minimize the impact of choosing failure. Almost always, we can embrace it as a learning opportunity.

The trick is to fail cheaply and early—and maybe often, make your mistakes, and move on. See what can be salvaged, what can be reinvented, and what should be thrown in the trash. Thomas Edison took 10,000 steps to invent the light bulb. Most people would say he failed 9999 times. He saw it not as a failure but as a 10,000-step process. In other words, our failures teach us enough to achieve our successes.

I've had my share of failures. This spring, for example, I set up a telesummit involving 17 speakers, plus eight bonus calls from my archives for those who purchased the recording package. I spent some money and a considerable amount of time.

And it failed.

The business model is proven. I just got a mailing from the organizer of another telesummit, and she reported 2500 signups and a 5% conversion to the paid recording package. If I'd had those numbers, I would have made a profit even after paying 50% commissions to the speakers who brought in those buyers. But I was not able to motivate people to visit, sign up, and buy.

What did she do differently? First, she had a much broader-based subject appeal. There are a lot more people who want to succeed as book authors than in running a green business. Second, she had more speakers. And third, she motivated all her participants with leaderboards and contests and a general sense that things were really moving and we all would want to get on the bandwagon.

While I was expecting a revenue stream instead of a cost center, I learned enormously from this failure. Among other things, I learned not to count on your speakers promoting your event in a meaningful way. Some of the largest list owners never mailed, and thus my traffic was far lower than expected. Low enough that the sales were basically invisible.

Here are some of my other takeaways:

1) Learn when to work with off-the-shelf products and when to go custom. I could have done 90 percent of what I wanted to with an off-the-shelf software package

called Instant Teleseminar. But their model involves paying every month, forever—so instead, I just hired someone to build the functionality I was looking for. That decision led to some serious cost overruns, and I still didn't achieve all the functionality I wanted. If the summit had succeeded and I did a new one every six or 12 months, developing the in-house solution still would have been the right decision, because it would probably pay for itself around the fourth summit. But since I doubt I'll organize another series like this one—though I might very well reuse the content I created and rerun the series at some point—I should have just bought the product.

2)   Keep it simple! The website is beautiful, but it's too hard to use. I think it scared people off. I should have really improved the usability before I let it go live.

3)   Identify an audience of buyers. The woman who achieved that big telesummit success could draw from tens of millions of people who want to be successful published authors. While there are hundreds of thousands who want to run successful green businesses, maybe that isn't a critical mass, especially since I didn't have a direct channel to reach them.

4)   Keep the content focused. I think my series split its energy between being about marketing, generally, and being about green business success. This may not have been wise. Maybe I needed to push more of the marketing experts to speak specifically about applying their techniques in the green world.

Impossible is a Dare: Business For a **Better World**

Well into the 21st century, isn't it time to finally say goodbye to the big crises that hold our whole society back? We should no longer have to put up with hunger, poverty, war, violence, and catastrophic climate change.

And here comes the outcry: "we've always suffered with these things. It's impossible to make them go away."

Well, guess what: we actually already know how to eliminate or greatly reduce most of the biggest problems the world faces.

And consider this: we do hundreds of things every day that were considered "impossible" not all that long ago.

When my house was built, in 1743, we assumed that humans couldn't travel faster than the fastest horse. Yet the International Space Station hurtles astronauts through space at 17,247 miles per hour. When I was born, in 1956, most people—if they had a phone at all—shared one phone, tethered by a wire to a wall, for a whole household, or sometimes several households. Most people had never even seen a computer, let alone owned one. Music came into our houses on big vinyl platters or over a staticky, low-fidelity radio. Apartheid reigned over South Africa, Rhodesia, and the American

South, while communist dictatorships ruled Eastern Europe. And life expectancy was decades less than it is today.

Those are just a very few of the thousands of shifts we've made about what is possible, in less than 60 years.

In short, "impossible" is a mindset, a self-imposed limitation—and we can change it.

We've known this for years. Henry Ford said, "Whether you think you can do a thing or think you can't do a thing, you're right." Muhammad Ali put it this way: "Impossible is just a big word thrown around by small men who find it easier to live in the world they've been given than to explore the power they have to change it. Impossible is not a fact. It's an opinion. Impossible is not a declaration. It's a dare. Impossible is potential. Impossible is temporary. Impossible is nothing."

This quote struck me so deeply that I built my entire TEDx talk around it: www.business-for-a-better-world.com/tedtalks—and I'll bet if you spend 15 minutes listening to it, you'll be inspired.

A Personal Example

I have first-hand experience. Among several "impossible" achievements, I founded the mass movement that stopped a developer's plan to kill our local mountain by building a large housing project. While the "experts" were wringing their hands, we went out and got it done.

Here's a key insight: when you look deeply, a lot of the causes of hunger, poverty, war, violence, and catastrophic climate change turn out to be about resources: who uses how much, whether they're taken sustainably, how fairly they're distributed. When we address resources systemically, we're able to transform hunger and poverty into sufficiency, war and violence into peace, and catastrophic climate change into planetary balance—and helping individuals reclaim their power to actively create this better world.

And we actually know how to do this. We knew how to build near-zero net-energy buildings at least as far back as 1983. We understand how to significantly increase crop yields without using chemicals and without compromising quality. We've developed all sorts of conflict resolution techniques that don't involve shooting each other. And we know how to replace nearly all our fossil and nuclear fuels with the combination of clean, renewable energy and deep conservation, thus reversing the increase in greenhouse gases. We even know how to imitate nature's best engineers to achieve zero waste while developing stronger, lighter materials and incredible processes to o things like extract water out of fog, the way a certain beetle does.

Where we've gotten stuck, in other words, in not in the technology. It's in finding the political will to implement all this great stuff.

But now for the good news: we don't have to wait around for governments to get it done. *We can motivate the private sector, the business community, by showing them how to make a profit.* We've tried for too long to motivate social change through guilt and shame. Let's try the profit motive instead.

I intend to spend the next 10 to 15 years of my life creating this incredibly exciting world where humans can reach our potential without fear. Will you join me in this incredible journey?

Learn more at www.business-for-a-better-world.com

* * *

I enjoyed writing this column from 2010 to 2014, and I think I provided very high value for those who read it. Unfortunately, I never got enough markets to make the project economically viable.

As I move in the direction of helping companies see the value in solving problems like hunger, poverty, war, and climate catastrophe, I can no longer afford the luxury of doing this column for the few markets that subscribed. So this will be the last issue for a while.

I'd love to bring it back, if I can get to a minimum number of subscribers each paying just $10 per month. If you have possible markets for me, please drop me a line at shel AT greenandprofitable.com with the subject "Column Market."

Disclaimer: The very observant among you may notice that some examples come up more than once. Keep in mind that this ebook is a compilation of a monthly column that ran for four years. I have organized the columns by topic rather than chronologically here, and as a result, columns that may have been years apart end up close to each other in the same ebook. Yes, some examples are repeated, but they were inserted to make different points, at different times. Please also note that nothing in this ebook series should be taken as legal or professional advice, and as in any situation, your results may vary as you implement the tips and ideas.

About Shel Horowitz and
Business For a Better World

Green business profitability expert Shel Horowitz shows businesses how to profit both by going green and by addressing problems like hunger and poverty, war, violence, and catastrophic climate change. Active in both marketing and the environment since his teen years in the early 1970s, Shel is the award-winning author of eight books including long-running Amazon category bestseller _Guerrilla Marketing Goes Green_.

- ✓ As a consultant, Shel brings laser focus to turning problems into opportunities, opening new markets, and helping you identify potential partners.

- ✓ As a marketing and informational copywriter trained in journalism, Shel is known for his clear writing, ability to make technical concepts accessible, and his skill in telling "the story behind the story" to move people to action.

- ✓ As an international speaker and trainer, Shel combines dynamic vocal style with powerful graphics and gets his audiences actively involved. He's spoken at major business and environmental conferences in locations as diverse as Istanbul, Davos (Switzerland), and Honolulu.

After over a decade actively assisting green businesses with their marketing, Shel branched out in 2014 to help businesses seize profit opportunities in turning hunger and poverty into sufficiency, war and violence into peace, and catastrophic climate change into planetary balance—and helping individuals reclaim their power to actively create this better world.

Shel is happy to talk to you about helping in any of these areas. Reach him at 413-586-2388 (8 a.m. to 10 p.m. US Eastern Time), email shel AT greenandprofitable.com, or find him on Twitter @ShelHorowitz.

Shel also has a gift for you: a free copy of his ebook, *Painless Green: 111 Tips to Help the Environment, Lower Your Carbon Footprint, Cut Your Budget, and Improve Your Quality of Life—With No Negative Impact on Your Lifestyle.* To claim your free copy of this $9.95 ebook, visit PainlessGreenBook.com/earthday and use the code, G&Pebook.

One more set of gifts, FREE with your no-cost subscription to Shel Horowitz's monthly Clean and Green Newsletter:

- ✓ Seven Tips to Gain Marketing Traction as a Green Guerrilla

- ✓ Seven Weeks to a Greener Business: once a week for seven weeks, tips on going greener with printing, energy saving, waste reduction, water conservation, transportation, going deep-green, and of course, green marketing.

- ✓ Plus the informative monthly newsletter, published since 1997 and featuring a business tip or profile plus a book review each issue.

Sign up in the upper-right-hand corner at http://greenandprofitable.com.

www.ingramcontent.com/pod-product-compliance
Lightning Source LLC
Chambersburg PA
CBHW051900170526
45168CB00001B/185